Be Born in Us Today

Be Born in Us Today

Billy E. Simmons

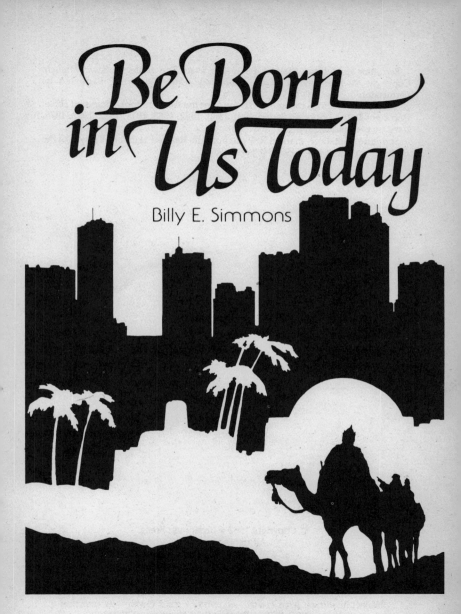

BROADMAN PRESS
Nashville, Tennessee

© Copyright 1982 ● Broadman Press.
All rights reserved.
4251-07
ISBN: 0-8054-5107-2

Dewey Decimal Classification: 232.92
Subject headings: JESUS CHRIST—NATIVITY / / JESUS CHRIST—INCARNATION
Library of Congress Catalog Card Number: 82-70047
Printed in the United States of America

This volume is dedicated
to the
many friends
who have shared
with me in the
ups and downs
of life.

Acknowledgments

Many people have had a share in the production of this little volume. Several of my friends and colleagues have encouraged me along the way, and I am grateful to them. I wish to thank especially my secretary, Mrs. Donna Dates, for her tireless labor in typing, proofing, and retyping the manuscript. Without her help, this project would not have come to fruition.

I am deeply indebted to the staff of Broadman Press for their constant encouragement on this matter.

I wish also to express appreciation to my family who have been patient with me during the months when it was necessary for me to be absent from family activities in order to meet a publishing deadline.

Preface

The coming of the sovereign God into human form is one of the major themes of the Christian faith. To affirm that this small volume has treated every facet of the incarnation would be a blatant overstatement indeed. The primary thrust here is simply to call attention to this important doctrine during the season of the year when we as Christians give most attention to it. There are, however, several meditations dealing with the incarnation from other than a Christmas perspective. This is to remind the reader that the doctrine of the incarnation is for every season and should not be relegated just to Christmas.

My prayer is that these simple meditations will bless the lives of those who read this volume. If in some small way this becomes a reality, my labor will have been well rewarded.

Contents

PART I
The Facts Surrounding the Incarnation

I
Foretelling the Incarnation

1 But there will be no more gloom for her who was in anguish; in earlier times He treated the land of Zebulun and the land of Naphtali with contempt, but later on He shall make it glorious, by the way of the sea, on the other side of Jordan, Galilee of the Gentiles.

2 The people who walk in darkness
Will see a great light;
Those who live in a dark land,
The light will shine on them.

3 Thou shalt multiply the nation,
Thou shalt increase their gladness;
They will be glad in Thy presence
As with the gladness of harvest,
As men rejoice when they divide the spoil.

4 For Thou shalt break the yoke of their burden
and the staff on their shoulders,
The rod of their oppressor, as at the battle of
Midian.

5 For every boot of the booted warrior in the
battle tumult,
And cloak rolled in blood, will be for burning,
fuel for the fire.

6 For a child will be born to us, a son will be
given to us;
And the government will rest on His shoulders;

> And His name will be called Wonderful
>   Counselor, Mighty God,
> Eternal Father, Prince of Peace.
> 7 There will be no end to the increase of His
>   government or of peace,
> On the throne of David and over his kingdom,
> To establish it and to uphold it with justice
>   and righteousness
> From then on and forevermore.
> The zeal of the Lord of hosts will accomplish
>   this.

(Isaiah 9:1-7, NASB)

Many and beautiful are the Old Testament prophecies that show foregleams of the coming of God in the flesh. Some of our loveliest hymns reflect the beauty of these passages. One of the grandest of these is "Come, Thou Long-Expected Jesus" by Charles Wesley. The first stanza has these words:

> Come, thou long-expected Jesus,
> Born to set thy people free;
> From our fears and sins release us;
> Let us find our rest in thee.
> Israel's strength and consolation,
> Hope of all the earth thou art;
> Dear desire of every nation,
> Joy of every longing heart.

The earliest Christians were sure that the Old Testament spoke of the coming of our Savior into the world. Jesus himself certified that the Old Testament testified of his coming. So when we think of the coming of the Lord Christ into the world, we do well to consider first of all the fact that his coming was foretold in the Old Testament.

The passage of Scripture quoted at the beginning of this chapter is one of the loveliest prophecies concerning the incarnation. In this passage, we can find several of the characteristics of the coming Prince of peace. Isaiah said that the coming of the Messiah would be like a bright light shining upon a darkened world. The blazing brightness of his purity will reveal the utter darkness of sin. John said in the prologue to his Gospel (John 1:5) that the darkness was not able to apprehend the light that was in Jesus. The world cannot cause the light of God's Son to stop shining. When the people who are walking in the darkness of sin look to the light that is in Christ, their darkness will be dispelled. They will truly come out of darkness into light.

The incarnate Son of God is the Light of the world, and he also brings joy to those who turn to him. As Isaac Watts wrote,

> Joy to the world! the Lord is come;
> Let earth receive her King; . . .
> And heav'n and nature sing,
> And heav'n and nature sing.

The joy that Christ brings is like the joy of harvest. To a land that depended for sustenance upon a bountiful harvest, this indeed is a great joy: the joy of anticipation and the joy of fulfillment.

Jesus also brings the joy of victory. The thrill that came to the victor dividing the spoils of war describes the sheer thrill of success. There is also joy when the burden of an oppressor is broken. Midian, the spoiler of the people of God, has been vanquished, and there is joy in the camp. The coming of the Messiah brings the joy of the breaking of sin's shackles upon his people. The joy of victory over the forces of evil belongs to us because of the fact that God has come to us in the person of Jesus Christ.

According to the prophecy, the incarnation would be accomplished in the birth of a child, in the giving of a son. Who is this child of destiny? What is his name? Isaiah said that "His name will be called Wonderful Counselor, Mighty God, Eternal Father, Prince of Peace." All of these are names that are worthy of the majesty of deity. Isaiah prophesied that God would come among his people in the person of a child upon whose shoulders the government would rest. This, however, was no ordinary government for, "There will be no end to the increase of His government or of peace." He will rule on the throne of David from the time of his coming and forevermore. "The zeal of the Lord of hosts will accomplish this."

If this were the only word provided for us in the Old Testament concerning the coming of the Son of God, it would be sufficient. We would need no other proof to convince us that God has been at work in salvation history bringing about his will. But there is more, so much more of the coming Incarnate One in the Old Testament that time or space will not permit the recitation of all of the prophecies. Yet, let me mention just a few more.

The first evangel of Genesis 3:15 records the first promise of God of the coming of One who will break the power of the serpent. The seed of woman ultimately will rise to bruise the serpent's head. Certainly this was accomplished in the coming of the Son of God as he defeated Satan in that cosmic conflict upon the cross.

In Deuteronomy 18:15, Moses told the people of Israel that God would raise up a prophet like himself. Though this is not one of the major messianic themes, the rabbis looked for the prophet of the end time who would be like Moses, and they identified him with Messiah. In the Gospel of Matthew, there are a number of parallels between Jesus and Moses that are more than just incidental. Matthew was saying to his readers that this prophet like unto Moses had come in Jesus.

God made a promise to David that his throne would be established forever (2 Sam. 7:16). From that point forward, there was never any doubt among the Jewish people that Messiah would be a descendant of David. The title Son of David was one of the most popular titles for Messiah during the time of Jesus. That God would come to his people was certain and that he would be of the seed of David was just as sure. When God came in the flesh, he was born into a family of the descendants of David.

Of all the Gospel writers, Matthew alone placed emphasis on the fact that Jesus' birth was according to prophecy. Perhaps this was due to the fact that his first reading audience was primarily Jewish. Whatever the reason, he saw the fulfillment of prophecy in several of the events surrounding the incarnation. He pointed to Micah 5:2 as the prophecy concerning the birthplace of Jesus. When the Wise Men came to Herod seeking the newborn king, he called the Jewish leaders to question them about the birthplace of the Messiah. They told him that Bethlehem was the place that had been prophesied by Micah.

Matthew pointed to Isaiah 7:14 as the prophecy concerning the virgin birth of our Lord. Because of this, his name was called Immanuel, which means God with us. What greater name could be given to the Christ child than this? What surer proof of the incarnation could there be than the fact that he truly is God with us?

> It came upon a midnight clear,
> That glorious song of old,
> From angels bending near the earth,
> To touch their harps of gold.
>
> For lo! the days are hast'ning on,
> By prophet bards foretold,

> When with the evercircling years
> Comes round the age of gold.
> (Edmund H. Sears)

The greatest miracle the world has ever known took place that night so many years ago in Bethlehem's manger. The eternal God became man. Nothing like it ever happened before, nor shall it ever happen again. The focal point of salvation history was recorded that night. The culmination of the plan of God for the salvation of men began to unfold in the little village of Bethlehem, and it was all "By prophet bards foretold."

2
Explaining the Incarnation

1 In the beginning was the Word, and the Word was with God, and the Word was God.

2 He was in the beginning with God.

3 All things came into being by Him; and apart from Him nothing came into being that has come into being.

4 In Him was life; and the life was the light of men.

5 And the light shines in the darkness; and the darkness did not comprehend it.

6 There came a man, sent from God, whose name was John.

7 He came for a witness, that he might bear witness of the light, that all might believe through him.

8 He was not the light, but came that he might bear witness of the light.

9 There was the true light which, coming into the world, enlightens every man.

10 He was in the world, and the world was made through Him, and the world did not know Him.

11 He came to His own, and those who were His own did not receive Him.

12 But as many as received Him, to them He gave the right to become children of God, even to those who believe in His name,

13 who were born not of blood, nor of the will of the flesh, nor of the will of man, but of God.

14 And the Word became flesh, and dwelt among us, and

we beheld His glory, glory as of the Only Begotten from the Father, full of grace and truth.
15 John bore witness of Him, and cried out, saying, "This was He of whom I said, 'He who comes after me has a higher rank than I, for He existed before me.'"
16 For of His fulness we have all received, and grace upon grace.
17 For the law was given through Moses; grace and truth were realized through Jesus Christ.
18 No man has seen God at any time; the only begotten God, who is in the bosom of the Father, He has explained Him.

(John 1:1-18, NASB)

Suppose that you are a person who knows nothing of Christ or of the way Americans celebrate Christmas. Imagine that you are spending the month of December in America, so that you might learn what Christmas really means. Your mission is to observe the way Americans celebrate Christmas, so that you might go back to your people and explain to them the true meaning of Christmas. What might you conclude on the basis of what you see and hear as Americans celebrate Christmas?

Of course, the Gospel records are our sources for the true meaning of Christmas. Each of the four Gospels deals differently with the birth of Christ. Mark does not tell of Christ's birth at all. Mark's Gospel begins with the ministry of Jesus. Luke tells of the announcement to Mary (1:26-38), of the birth of Jesus in Bethlehem (2:1-7), and of the coming of the shepherds (2:8-20). Matthew tells of the announcement to Joseph and of the coming of the Wise Men (2:1-23). John does not describe these events at all. Instead, he explains the meaning of these events. In a magnificent prologue (1:1-18), John begins with the preexistent Word of God and tells of his coming into the world as a man. This marvelous passage might be called a theological explanation of the incarnation. An understanding of John 1:1-18 will help us to comprehend the true basis of the incarnation.

The Preexistent Word (John 1:1-5)

The first five verses of John's Gospel contain some of the most sublime thoughts to be found anywhere in the Bible. They point to the preexistent state of the eternal Word. He was not a created being, but he existed prior to creation. In fact, it was he who brought about creation.

Matthew began with a genealogy looking back to Abraham, and Luke used a genealogy which goes back to Adam. John begins with a sweeping statement that is strikingly similar to the beginning of Genesis: "In the beginning was the Word." This alerts us to the fact that John was dealing with the vastness of the meaning of his coming.

The "Word" is a reference to the preexistent Christ, and it is a translation of the Greek *logos.* This word was used by the Greek philosophers such as Heraclitus and Plato to refer to various sublime principles in the universe. Philo of Alexandria, a Jewish philosopher, also used the word *logos* quite a bit in his writings, but not with the same meaning found here. None of these writers ever gave the *logos* personality as did John.

The "Word" was also a familiar term among the Hebrews. In the Greek Old Testament the word *logos* is used to render the Hebrew term *dabar,* which also means word or principle. The Hebrews thought of a word as an active expression of a person's personality. Thus "the word of the Lord" in the Old Testament is often used as an active expression of God's person and purpose. For example, in the Genesis account God's spoken word brought the world into being. Often in the prophetic literature as well as in the Samuel and Kings materials the "Word of the Lord" came through prophetic spokesmen with a direct message from God.

When John used the phrase "the word was with God," he was indicating that the preexistent Word was not a created being of lesser rank but rather shared the eternal nature of God. In the Greek of John's day the phrase was used to describe men of equal rank or dignity. Sometimes the phrase is translated "the word was face-to-face with God" to preserve the idea that in his preexistent state, the Word was coeternal with God, the Father.

The phrase cannot be reversed to read "God was the Word," nor can it be rendered "the word was a god." In this clause, the definite article before God is not present in the Greek text. The construction used means the word *God* could well be translated "Deity." When the article is present, the Father God is meant. Thus in another clause, "and the Word was with God," the definite article is present in the Greek text. The phrase "and the Word was God" means that the eternal Word possessed the qualities of Deity. He was not all there was of God, but he possessed all of the qualities of God. The Word who was with God and who shared the very nature of God was in the beginning with God. This statement is repeated in order to introduce his work of creation mentioned in verse 3. Not only was Christ present with the Father in his preexistent state, he was also active in the work of creation. He was not just active in creation; he was the agent in all of creation. There was nothing created that he did not create. All of the universe in its several parts is the result of his creative work. The Word was not a created being. He was the divine agent in creation, and as such the life principle resided in him. All of life, whether physical or spiritual, came from him. He is the source and giver of all life.

As the preexistent Word imparted life physically and spiritually to men, he also was the source of all that could be called good. He is the light. For light represents good in John's Gospel. The goodness coming from the preexistent Word is not just a glimmer in the darkness. Rather, it is a steady stream of light that "goes on shining in the darkness" (Basic).

The idea of comprehending or understanding may be the meaning in verse 5. It is certainly true that the darkness is not able to understand the way of the light. However, the more likely meaning here is not to understand but to overcome. Just as light penetrates and expels darkness, so goodness is more powerful than evil. Evil cannot overcome the good; though it may appear at times that the evil has triumphed, it will not ultimately be victorious.

John's statement concerning the preexistent Word and his creative activity in these verses should be compared with Paul's statement in Colossians 1:15-17. Both passages present a very high and positive view of Christ. In verses 1-5 John alerted his readers to the fact that he was interested in explaining the meaning of the coming of Christ.

The Witness of John (John 1:6-8)

In these verses the writer contrasted the ministry of John the Baptist with that of Jesus. Jesus was the light; John was sent to bear witness to the light. No doubt was left in the minds of the readers as to the distinctiveness of their ministries. As great a work as John the Baptist did, he was not to be confused with Jesus and his task. John the Baptist was not the Christ, the divine Light. He was only a man. However, he was a man sent from God with a mission to perform.

The basic reason for John's ministry was to point to someone else. He was not to draw attention to himself; rather, he was to bear testimony to Jesus. John had no message to bring except that of the One who was to come after him. The effectiveness of his ministry would be gauged by the people that he pointed to Jesus.

The writer was emphatic at this point concerning the ministry of John the Baptist. His ministry was to point men to the light so that through his witness others could believe in the One who was the light. John the Baptist was a man sent from God for a purpose, but he was just that and no more. He was not the Messiah.

In just a few short statements, the author has presented in no uncertain terms his assessment of John the Baptist. He was a good man. He was sent from God for a particular mission. His mission was to point to Jesus as the Messiah. He was not to be mistaken for the Messiah. Rather, he was a witness pointing to the Messiah so that all might trust through him.

Man's Reaction to the Word (John 1:9-13)

In these verses, the reactions of humanity to the coming of the eternal Word into the world are briefly highlighted. Though some did receive him, many rejected him. Even though the Word created the world and mankind, many people would not accept him. To those who did receive him, however, he gave the authority to become God's children.

In the Gospel of John there are certain key words. The word *true* is one of these. The meaning is not so much that of truth as opposed to falseness. Instead, it refers to the real, as opposed to the unreal. Jesus was not an imitation light. He was the real thing!

"Light" in the New Testament signifies more than intellectual enlightenment. It is often used as a description of salvation (see Col. 1:12-14). In John 1 "light" refers to God's revelation in Christ as the One through whom we become children of God.

Some take the phrase "coming into the world" as a qualifying phrase for "every man." This would give a drastically different meaning to the statement. Though it is a difficult passage to render, the translation in the Revised Standard Version appears to be a very good one.

Again John emphasizes the creative power of Jesus. As the Creator of the world, Christ came into his own creation.

Verse 11*b* is a most tragic statement. Though he created the world and everything in it, the world did not know him. Often in John's Gospel the word *world* has reference to that segment of humanity which has consciously set itself against God and his purposes.

Verse 10 refers to Christ's rejection by the people he had created. Verse 11 refers to his rejection by that segment of humanity that was distinctly his own. Not only did the people of the world at large reject him, but many of his own people rejected him. Thus many of those who had been especially prepared for his coming refused him.

The rejection, however, was not universal. Some (including both Jews and Gentiles) accepted him for what he was. They believed in his name. In ancient times a person's name was significant, for it revealed the person's character. If a person grew to maturity and his name did not reflect his character, he quite often was given a nickname that did describe his character (see John 1:42). The name *Jesus* was given to him because of his vocation as Savior (Matt. 1:21). The name means Jehovah will save. So when a person believes in the name of Jesus, he accepts Jesus as Savior.

God's ultimate gift of grace to mankind is the authority to become his children. In some general sense, all people are potentially the children of God by virtue of creation. At least God has a fatherly concern for all. However, the Bible makes salvation, not creation, the basis for being children of God. The image of God in man has been so marred by sin that spiritual re-creation is necessary for one to become a true child of God.

The miracle of re-creation cannot be effected by man under any circumstances. A man's bloodline or race has nothing to do with this act of God's grace. There is no way that man can bring this about through natural generation.

For this miracle to occur in a person's life, God must become operative in his life. As God brought about the first creation, so he must also be active in the new creation. As it took an act of God to bring the world and man into being, so it will also take an act of God to re-create man and efface the marred image.

How any man could say so much in such a short space and in such simple language has been a mystery since the time that John penned his Gospel. Yet in just a few brief sentences he has given man's reaction to the coming of Christ. For many it was a time of rejection. For others, however, it meant receiving Christ for what he truly is. To these he gave the greatest gift of God's grace. He restored what Adam lost. He took the image of God, marred by sin, and restored it to its former beauty. He gave those who received him the authority to become God's children.

The Significance of the Incarnation
(John 1:14-18)

In these verses John sets forth his statement concerning the incarnation. As can be seen from this paragraph, the writer did not dwell on the historical facts surrounding the birth of Jesus; instead, he was interested in the meaning of these facts. Though the language is very simple, the thoughts are quite deep.

The writer used a different verb in verse 14 to describe Jesus' coming in the flesh than he used in verse 1 to describe his preexistent state. The term *was* is found in verse 1, but the term *became* is found in verse 14. At a specific point in history the eternal Word became flesh.

John may have used the word *flesh* in order to refute a popular misunderstanding of the incarnation. A group of people, called Gnostics in later times, disputed the fact that Jesus was human. They said he only seemed or appeared to be human. As far as they were concerned, flesh was inherently evil; therefore, God could not allow himself to be clothed in flesh. John was probably writing to combat this heresy when he said, "And the Word became flesh." Thus the word *flesh* underscores the reality of the humanity of Jesus Christ. The eternal Word became a person, and he came to live in the world of people.

In his incarnate state, our Lord was the epitome of grace. In John's Gospel, truth generally refers to what is real as opposed to what is unreal. So, in his incarnate state, Jesus was the genuine representative of the grace of God.

The word *beheld* in verse 14 means to gaze upon intently. In the First Epistle of John, this idea is expanded to further combat the Gnostics. There John wrote about Jesus in terms very much like those used here in his Gospel.

When John said "and we beheld His glory" what did he mean? Surely it is difficult to say precisely to what he referred. Possibly he was referring to the transfiguration of Jesus. He also may have been referring to that spiritual splendor which was seen in Jesus Christ throughout the entire incarnation. Whatever the case, John was affirming that he was an eyewitness to the incarnation.

The word *fullness* was a word used often by the Gnostics to refer to the completeness of what they thought of as God. They believed the fullness consisted of many semidivine beings and that Jesus was among the lower ranks of these beings. John affirmed that Jesus was much more than this. The "fulness" resided in Jesus. In writing to the Colossian Christians, Paul made what is perhaps the strongest statement concerning this very matter in Colossians 2:9.

The phrase "grace upon grace" indicates a never-ending supply of grace. Literally, it is "grace over against grace." From whatever perspective one may view it, there is an abundance of grace. God never runs short.

The law was an important part of God's revelation. When God was ready to reveal his law, he chose Moses, a great man, to be the recipient and the mediator of that revelation.

When God wanted to reveal himself to man, he became a man. The law was given through a great man, but grace and truth came in the person of Jesus Christ, the God-man. In his person he embodied grace and truth.

When John said that no one has seen God, he had in mind physical sight. God is Spirit, immortal, eternal, and invisible. Therefore man cannot know God through his physical senses. However, through the incarnation, he has revealed himself to man so that man can better know and comprehend what God is like. The phrase "bosom of the Father" implies the closest and most intimate fellowship. Jesus and the Father are indeed one.

The idea in the Hebrew concept of "Son" stresses the likeness of Jesus Christ the Son to God the Father. God has made himself known in the life of his Son, who is both God and man. (See Heb. 1:1-3.) The point made in the first part of verse 18 is that man cannot discover or know God on his own. The last part of verse 18 emphasizes that God has graciously chosen to make himself known in Jesus Christ.

Conclusion

The One who entered the world at Bethlehem's stable was the eternal Word of God.—His earthly sojourn began at that specific time and place in history; however, in essence he is eternal. He was in the beginning with God; he shares the very nature of God. He is not a created being; on the contrary, he shared in the creation of all things.

The eternal Word of God became flesh.—That is, he became a real person. He was still uniquely the Son of God, but he also was a human being. This is the mystery of the incarnation. Jesus Christ is God and man. He is not less than God, nor is he less than man. He is the God-man.

He came in order to make God known.—A word is a means of communication, the way a person reveals himself and his thoughts. God has used many and varied ways of making himself known to man, but God's clearest revelation is in Jesus Christ. When God wanted to speak his clearest word to humanity, he did so in the life of a human being. Christians do not say, "We believe Jesus is God's Son because he is so much like God." Rather we say, "We believe God is as he is revealed to be in Jesus Christ." Jesus is our primary source for what we know of God's nature and purpose.

The Word came as saving light so that men might become the children of God.—God's nature is seen in what God does. His saving acts are seen in Jesus' coming, life, death, and resurrection. Those who believe in Jesus Christ come to know personally the saving power and gracious presence of God. The true meaning of Christ's coming cannot be known until one receives Jesus Christ as his personal Lord and Savior.

3
Preparing for the Incarnation

26 Now in the sixth month the angel Gabriel was sent from God to a city in Galilee, called Nazareth,

27 to a virgin engaged to a man whose name was Joseph, of the descendants of David; and the virgin's name was Mary.

28 And coming in, he said to her, "Hail, favored one! The Lord is with you."

29 But she was greatly troubled at this statement, and kept pondering what kind of salutation this might be.

30 And the angel said to her, "Do not be afraid, Mary; for you have found favor with God.

31 "And behold, you will conceive in your womb, and bear a son, and you shall name Him Jesus.

32 "He will be great, and will be called the Son of the Most High; and the Lord God will give Him the throne of His father David;

33 and He will reign over the house of Jacob forever; and His kingdom will have no end."

34 And Mary said to the angel, "How can this be, since I am a virgin?"

35 And the angel answered and said to her, "The Holy Spirit will come upon you, and the power of the Most High will overshadow you; and for that reason the holy offspring shall be called the Son of God.

(Luke 1:26-35, NASB)

18 Now the birth of Jesus Christ was as follows. When His mother Mary had been betrothed to Joseph, before they came together she was found to be with child by the Holy Spirit.

19 And Joseph her husband, being a righteous man, and not wanting to disgrace her, desired to put her away secretly.

20 But when he had considered this, behold, an angel of the Lord appeared to him in a dream, saying, "Joseph, son of David, do not be afraid to take Mary as your wife; for that which has been conceived in her is of the Holy Spirit.

21 "And she will bear a Son; and you shall call His name Jesus, for it is He who will save His people from their sins."

22 Now all this took place that what was spoken by the Lord through the prophet might be fulfilled, saying,

23 "Behold, the virgin shall be with child, and shall bear a Son, and they shall call His name Immanuel."

(Matthew 1:18-23, NASB)

Today when a family is expecting the birth of a child, elaborate preparations are made. A doctor is retained. Plans are made for the long-awaited journey to the hospital. A nursery is prepared at home and stocked with all of the essentials needed in caring for the newborn infant.

Though the preparations for Jesus' birth were somewhat different, they were nontheless unique. God prepared the way for the coming of his Son into the World. Mary and Joseph had to have their minds and hearts prepared for this great event. That is what this chapter is all about.

In Luke's account of the birth narrative, attention is given to Mary and her reaction to the blessed event. The passage deals with the angel's announcement to her and her reaction to it. Luke presented her as a humble, pious, young woman who received God's gracious blessing of being the mother of the Son of God. When the angel made this announcement to Mary, she was astonished, and she asked how this could be. The angel then told her of the miracle that would be worked in her through the Holy Spirit. Her response to this announcement was submissive trust and obedience.

Matthew's account of these events focuses on Joseph and his reaction to the announcement of this miraculous event. Mary had been betrothed to Joseph. This was somewhat like our engagement but more binding. According to their custom, a betrothal could be dissolved only by divorce. When Joseph became aware that Mary was pregnant, he decided to divorce her as quietly as possible. The fact that he did not want to make a public spectacle of Mary shows the kindness of the man. While Joseph was giving consideration to these matters, an angel revealed to him what was taking place. He was told of the miracle of divine conception and of the nature of Jesus' mission as Savior. The statement of the angel was reinforced by a statement from Isaiah 7:14, which was now to be fulfilled in the virgin birth.

The Announcement to Mary (Luke 1:26-33)

Here we find a record of the announcement of the angel Gabriel to Mary concerning the birth of Jesus. Mary had been betrothed to Joseph and was looking forward to their approaching marriage. When the announcement came, she was living in the village of Nazareth in Galilee. She was alone at the time, and the angel assured her that she had found favor with God. He also told her that she would conceive and bear a son, and he further instructed her that she should call his name Jesus.

Gabriel is mentioned in Luke 1:19 as the messenger to Zacharias concerning the birth of John the Baptist. Also, he is the angel who came to Daniel with messages from God (Dan. 9:21). Whether or not the statement in Luke 1:19 "I am Gabriel, who stands in the presence of God" marks him as a special class of angels is uncertain. Standing in God's presence could probably be said of all angels. Yet this statement does appear to single him out in some particular way. At any rate, it can be said that he was entrusted by God with special messages.

The little village of Nazareth nestled in the hills of Galilee just a short distance from the Sea of Galilee was home for Mary and Joseph. They had to make the difficult seventy-five-mile journey to the village of Bethlehem (the birthplace of Jesus) during the census, and they evidently lived there for some time after our Lord's birth. Eventually, however, they returned to Nazareth to rear their family (Matt. 2:23; Luke 2:39).

Both Matthew and Luke emphasize the fact of the virgin birth. This is an indication that the early church believed and taught the virgin birth to their converts. The accounts of apostolic preaching in the Book of Acts major on the death and resurrection of Jesus rather than on the manner of his birth. This shows that the virgin birth was not a vital part of the evangelistic witness to lost people. There is little doubt, however, that belief in the virgin birth was part of the faith of those who had come to know the crucified, risen Lord. The prominence of the teaching in Matthew and Luke testifies to this. The nature of the teaching was such that it would easily have been misunderstood by non-

Christians. Thus the facts about the manner of Jesus' birth were probably a part of the church's teaching to believers, not a part of its proclamation to unbelievers.

A betrothal usually lasted a year, and it was a legally binding contract. This agreement could be dissolved only by a divorce action instituted by the man involved.

Joseph could trace his ancestry back to David. This statement is significant, for it prepared the way for Joseph and Mary's trip to Bethlehem as recorded in Luke 2:1-5. Also the Jews believed that the Messiah was to be born of the lineage of David. (See 2 Sam. 7:13; Isa. 9:7.)

The angel Gabriel made the announcement to Mary. His first words were words of assurance. The word *favored* is built on the same root as the word for grace. Even in this activity, God was taking the initiative. He continued by assuring her that the Lord was with her.

Mary was "troubled" by Gabriel's statement. In addition to its obvious meaning, this word also can mean confused or perplexed. The appearance of Gabriel was, to say the least, an unusual experience for Mary. The fact that he would greet such a humble maiden as she in such glowing terms was further cause for her confusion. She had never encountered such a being before. Therefore, she was naturally concerned about the meaning of his greeting. She began to turn the words over in her mind, trying to come to some conclusion about the matter. By this time Mary was certainly aware that Gabriel was no ordinary visitor. Naturally she was afraid, so the angel reassured her that she need not be afraid. The angel assured her again that God had smiled on her. The word translated "favored" is actually the same word translated "grace" in other contexts. Again the impact of the statement appears to be that the sovereign God had taken the initiative in this matter.

Mary had not planned this and come to God about it; rather God in his grace had planned this and sent his angel to tell Mary.

This is the first hint of what Gabriel had come to announce to Mary. She had been wondering in her heart what this unusual messenger might tell her. Now she would know.

Both Luke and Matthew record the fact that Jesus' name was decreed by angelic announcement. Matthew 1:21 tells of the significance of Jesus' name.

After Gabriel had announced to Mary the fact that she would bear a son, he continued with a description of his person. Mary's child was to be the very Son of God. In him would come to fruition the promise that God made to David. He was to be the true descendant of David. He was to be the fulfillment of ancient prophecies of the Messiah to the descendants of Israel. The word *kingdom* might be translated "rule" just as well. His rule was to be an eternal one.

Thus in verses 26-33, Luke alerted his readers to the fact that the birth of Jesus was no ordinary event. It was preceded by an angelic announcement. The one who was to be the mother of the Messiah was a humble, young virgin from a village in Galilee. In the course of the announcement Mary was told that her child would be called the Son of God.

Mary's Reaction (Luke 1:34-37)

Mary's immediate reaction to the angelic announcement was one of confusion. Because of this, the angel reassured her and told her how the miracle was to take place within her. The Holy Spirit would come upon her in such power that she would conceive and bear a son.

Mary had been confronted by an angel representing the realm of the supernatural. He had told her of a miracle involving her in the birth of a child, who was to be the Son of God. Mary's question was not evidence of a lack of faith; she asked a natural question under the circumstances. "How can this be?"

She was a chaste virgin, and she was unmarried. How was this child to be conceived? She no doubt knew the stories of other supernatural interventions in bringing about the birth of children. The birth of Isaac in the Old Testament was the best known of such miracles. Mary also was soon to learn of the unusual circumstances related to the pregnancy of her kinswoman Elizabeth (Luke 1:36). An angel was involved in the announcement of this birth also (Luke 1:5-25). However, in the case of these and other similar miraculous births, human conception always had involved a man and a woman.

In other words, this conception was not to take place by natural processes of procreation. Hers was to be a miraculous conception presided over by the Holy Spirit of God. The eternal, immortal, invisible God was going to become incarnate. He would come as a man-child and grow to maturity as other men had done.

Though Mary was shocked by the announcement and appeared almost incredulous, the angel assured her that what he had said would take place through the miraculous intervention of the Holy Spirit. He was going to intervene in the natural life processes and cause Mary to conceive and bear a man-child. This child would be holy; in fact, he would be God's Son.

In verses 36-37, the angel alerted Mary to the fact that her cousin Elizabeth was in the sixth month of her pregnancy. This was a near-miraculous conception, for Elizabeth was beyond the normal age of childbearing. This additional information seems to have been given to reassure Mary that God would do this marvelous thing with her.

Verses 36-37 do not mean that the miracle of John's birth was in the same exact category as the miracle of Jesus' birth. The biblical record makes plain that only Jesus was born of a virgin. However, John's birth was miraculous. So the angel used this to remind Mary that God could intervene in a miraculous way in order to accomplish his will. He could give a son to Zacharias and Elizabeth after the age of childbearing was passed. He also could miraculously cause a child to be conceived in a virgin.

Mary's response in verse 38 is indeed a beautiful one. "Behold the bondslave of the Lord; be it done to me according to your word." She was submissive to the will of God. She knew that this pregnancy could well be misunderstood by Joseph and others. However, she was willing to let the Lord have his way in her life.

Joseph's Discovery (Matthew 1:18-19)

Matthew presents the account of Jesus' birth from the perspective of Joseph. Joseph was a man of humble birth, and he lived in Nazareth of Galilee. Before the time that he and Mary were to be married, he discovered that she was pregnant. Joseph determined to divorce her as quietly as possible, but his plans were changed when an angel appeared to him in a dream. The angel assured him that Mary's pregnancy was the work of the Holy Spirit. He was not to be afraid to take her as his wife. Furthermore, the angel instructed him that he should call the child "Jesus." Then he quoted a reference from Isaiah 7:14 to reinforce the fact that the Messiah was to be born of a virgin.

Matthew 1:1-18 traces the genealogy of Jesus. The first part of verse 18 was Matthew's way of alerting the reader to the fact that he was beginning the birth narrative. This is how it all came about.

Both Matthew and Luke stress the fact that Mary was betrothed to Joseph. According to the customs of the time, Mary had little if anything to say about this. Usually parents made the marriage arrangements. Mary may have been quite a bit younger than Joseph. Joseph does not appear in the biblical record after the time when Jesus was twelve years old (Luke 2:41-52). Very likely Joseph died before the beginning of Jesus' ministry.

The Jewish betrothal was a more binding agreement than an engagement in our society. If the man died, the woman was considered a widow. Also, a divorce was necessary to break the agreement. However, the betrothed pair did not live together as husband and wife; thus Mary was still a virgin.

The statement that Mary "was found to be with child by the Holy Spirit" is the first reference in Matthew's Gospel to the miraculous nature of Jesus' conception. Matthew does not record the angelic announcement to Mary. At this point Mary, but not Joseph, was aware of the miracle. She knew that she was with child of the Holy Spirit, but at this moment Joseph knew nothing of this. When he discovered that she was to have a child, Joseph had no choice but to assume that Mary had been unfaithful to him. Though Joseph was not yet technically her husband, he nevertheless had responsibilities in this matter just as though he were her husband. Both Mary and Joseph were people of simple, sincere faith who were anxious to do what was right and good. Joseph wanted to be both just and fair in this matter. He felt obligated to set aside their marriage agreement, but he wanted to avoid subjecting Mary to any shame. This shows that he was "just," not in the sense of seeking retribution. He was not a vindictive man. Rather, his sense of justice was combined with mercy and concern. He was a truly good man.

Divorce proceedings among the Jews of the first century could be handled privately. A man could bring charges against his wife quietly and give her a written statement of divorce. The woman had no legal recourse but to accept this decree. Joseph had no intention of making a public spectacle of Mary. He planned to take care of the matter quietly. Then something happened that made him change his mind.

The Announcement to Joseph (Matthew 1:20-23)

Joseph did not desire to take any rash or hasty action. During the time that he was considering what action he should take, an angel appeared to him in a dream. The angel told him to give up his divorce plans and take Mary as his wife according to his original plans. The angel assured him that the child was conceived of the Holy Spirit.

Just as Mary was given definite instructions concerning the name of the child, so was Joseph. "For it is He who will save His people from their sins" (NASB) is an added explanation that was not given to Mary in the angelic announcement. The name *Jesus* is the Greek form of the Hebrew name *Joshua.* It means "Jehovah will save." Thus the name of this child has great significance. In fact it outlines, in brief, his mission upon the earth.

The Greek word here for *virgin* means exactly what the Greek version of the Old Testament, which also had the word *virgin* in Isaiah 7:14, intended. The Hebrew word in Isaiah 7:14 means simply a young woman who has no husband. In its original context, the Isaiah 7:14 statement had to do with a sign that was to be given to King Ahaz by the Lord. Thus the prophecy, like many other Old Testament prophecies, may have had an immediate and an ultimate fulfillment. Whatever the immediate fulfillment of Isaiah 7:14 may have been, Matthew 1:23 leaves little doubt that Matthew considered the virgin birth of our Lord as the ultimate fulfillment of this prophecy. God was to come in human form and abide with man. This was not merely visual appearance. This was really God coming in the form of human flesh to redeem us from our sins.

In the final two verses of chapter 1, Matthew recounts Joseph's action after the angel appeared to him in the dream. He followed the angel's instructions and married Mary. There was, however, no physical consummation of the marriage until after Jesus was born.

Conclusion

Mary and Joseph were humble people of genuine faith and goodness.—Significantly, Jesus was not born to the high and mighty of his day. He was not born in the king's palace or in the high priest's mansion. Jesus was born to Mary, a young woman of the common people of the land. Joseph, her betrothed, was a carpenter. Both were people of deep and sincere faith in God. Both were people of deep righteousness and goodness. God deliberately chose people like Mary and Joseph to care for the child Jesus. This says something about God's purpose in sending his Son.

The virgin birth of Jesus is clearly taught in the New Testament.—Mary and Joseph knew that this was a miracle, and so did Matthew, Luke, and other early Christians. The examples of early Christian preaching recorded in Acts (also written by Luke) make no mention of the virgin birth. Most of those sermons were proclamations of Jesus' death and resurrection aimed at evangelizing the lost. Apparently the virgin birth was not included in evangelistic sermons to unbelieving people. However, the virgin birth was a part of what was taught to converts. Its inclusion in Matthew 1 and Luke 1 shows that this was true. An unbeliever might easily misunderstand this teaching, but a person who had come to trust Jesus Christ as the crucified, risen Lord could appreciate the impact of the miracle of the miraculous conception and virgin birth.

The manner of Jesus' birth testifies to his unique nature as Emmanuel.—The fact that Jesus was born to the virgin Mary emphasizes that Jesus is the Son of God. This fact does not deny that he was human as well as divine. He was born of a virgin, but he was born. He did not spring full grown to earth. The virgin-born child was the Word made flesh, Emmanuel.

The virgin birth also points to Jesus' mission as Savior. The power of God is seen in the miracle of his coming. As God was able to do the impossible in this birth, so is he able to save sinners. In this sense, the virgin birth of Jesus is a sign of the spiritual new birth. Matthew 1:21 makes explicit the saving mission implicit in the coming of Jesus.

4
Responding to the Incarnation

1 Now after Jesus was born in Bethlehem of Judea in the days of Herod the king, behold, magi from the east arrived in Jerusalem, saying,

2 "Where is He who has been born King of the Jews? For we saw His star in the east, and have come to worship Him."

3 And when Herod the king heard it, he was troubled, and all Jerusalem with him.

4 And gathering together all the chief priests and scribes of the people, he began to inquire of them where the Christ was to be born.

5 And they said to him, "In Bethlehem of Judea, for so it has been written by the prophet,

6 'And you, Bethlehem, Land of Judah,
   Are by no means least among the leaders of Judah;
   For out of you shall come forth a Ruler,
   Who will shepherd My people Israel.'"

7 Then Herod secretly called the magi, and ascertained from them the time the star appeared.

8 And he sent them to Bethlehem, and said, "Go and make careful search for the Child; and when you have found Him, report to me, that I too may come and worship Him."

9 And having heard the king, they went their way; and lo, the star, which they had seen in the east, went on

before them, until it came and stood over where the Child was.

10 And when they saw the star, they rejoiced exceedingly with great joy.

11 And they came into the house and saw the Child with Mary His mother; and they fell down and worshiped Him; and opening their treasures they presented to Him gifts of gold and frankincense and myrrh.

12 And having been warned by God in a dream not to return to Herod, they departed for their own country by another way.

13 Now when they departed, behold, an angel of the Lord appeared to Joseph in a dream, saying, "Arise and take the Child and His mother, and flee to Egypt, and remain there until I tell you; for Herod is going to search for the Child to destroy Him."

14 And he arose and took the Child and His mother by night, and departed for Egypt;

15 and was there until the death of Herod, that what was spoken by the Lord through the prophet might be fulfilled, saying "Out of Egypt did I call My Son."

(Matthew 2:1-15, NASB)

The joy of Christmas should be more than a seasonal emphasis in a Christian's life. There should be a commitment on the part of all Christians to worship and serve the Lord in a spirit of joy throughout the year.

As Matthew recorded this incident surrounding the birth narrative of Jesus, he introduced the reader to a group of people seldom mentioned in the Bible. The Wise Men came from the East to worship the newborn King. Their coming shows that Jesus Christ came to redeem the whole world of men, not just a narrow segment of it, and they are representative of the world outside of Palestine.

They approached Herod's palace, thinking that one of the royal lineage would be born there. This was a normal action since they were looking for one who was born to the king. The king's response to their coming introduces the reader to the rejection that would be a part of our Lord's lot throughout his ministry. Herod's reaction was as negative as the Wise Men's response was positive.

The Wise Men (Matthew 2:1-2)

Matthew's allusion to Herod places the birth of Jesus in historical context, alerting the reader to the situation at the time of Jesus' birth. Roman rule had begun in Palestine in 63 BC. Herod was not of royal blood. However, he had managed to have the Romans declare him king of the Jews in 37 BC.

Herod the Great, as he came to be called, was ruthless and unscrupulous. One of his first acts was to exterminate all those of the real royal blood. He not only had his favorite wife put to death because of jealousy, he also had three of his sons executed because he thought they were trying to steal his throne. As the years passed, he became even more insanely jealous of his throne and was suspicious of anyone who even remotely appeared to challenge his position as king of the Jews. With this in mind, we can understand his actions as recorded by Matthew. What he did fits the total pattern of his life.

The word translated "wise men" is rather obscure. The word can mean magician or astrologer. It was also applied to the priestly caste in Persia. Where these men were from cannot be accurately determined. All we are told is that they were "from the east." They were probably from either

Persia or Babylon. During Old Testament times the Jews came into contact with both the Babylonians and the Persians. A large colony of Jews remained in Babylon even after the Exile was ended. This could explain how the Wise Men became interested in the promised King of the Jews.

The Wise Men apparently knew little about Herod at this point except that he was the ruling king of the Jews. They seem to have assumed that the one born King of the Jews was born in Herod's palace. This was a logical assumption for them to make.

There is nothing bizarre about Matthew's claim that a star arose to herald the birth of the King of kings and guided the Wise Men from the East in their quest to find him. Many ancients believed that a new star appeared in the heavens to mark an important event. Vergil in *The Aeneid* (II, 694) reports that a star guided Aeneas to the exact spot where Rome was to be established. Josephus in *The Wars of the Jews* (VI, v, 3) speaks of a star "resembling a sword" which stood over the city of Jerusalem and "a comet that continued a whole year" at the time of the fall of the city. The Roman historian Pliny in his *Natural History* (II, v1, 28) seeks to refute the opinion popular in his day that every person has a star that starts to give light on the day of his birth and fades out when the person dies. This is evidence that such a belief among the ancients was widespread. Roman history records a number of instances where the birth of a king was presaged by the appearance of new stars in the heavens. So it was at the birth of Jesus. Just what brilliant star these men saw is not known. Several suggestions have been put forward by men who have studied the astronomical phenomena that occurred during the years surrounding Jesus' birth. At least since the time of Johannes Kepler who lived during the seventeenth century there have been detailed studies by astronomers of peculiar events in the heavens during the decade prior to the birth of Jesus (14-4 BC). Since it is known beyond any doubt that Herod the Great died in 4 BC, Jesus was born prior to that year.

The Adler Planetarium of Chicago has published a brochure entitled "The Star of Bethlehem." This brochure discusses three proposals which have been made by astronomers concerning the star which presaged the birth of our Savior.

Kepler suggested that what the Magi saw was a super nova or a new star. This occurs when a faint or distant star explodes, thus giving out a great deal of light for weeks or even months before it subsides. Super nova so bright that they could be seen in daylight have been recorded. None, however, is known to have occurred in the ten years prior to Jesus' birth.

Others have suggested that what the Magi saw was a comet. A comet moves in a regular elliptical orbit around the sun. When in the distant part of its orbit, a comet cannot be seen from earth. However, when it comes near the earth, it can have a striking appearance—particularly if it has a luminous tail consisting of gases and dust.

The particular comet that has been associated with Jesus' birth is the one known as Halley's. This comet is visible from earth every seventy-seven years. By astronomical calculations, astronomers have found that this comet was visible from earth in 12-11 BC. It made its last appearance in 1911. According to one biblical scholar who was living in Jerusalem in 1911, it came from the East. While it was overhead, it faded out—only to reappear several days later as it set in the West. However, since a comet was usually associated with a coming catastrophic event it likely would not have been associated with the birth of a king.

The third suggestion that has been made by astronomers is a planetary conjunction. It is known that a conjunction of the planets Saturn, Jupiter, and Mars occurs every 805 years. The last occurrence was in October 1604, recorded by Johannes Kepler. This same planetary conjunction occurred in 7-6 BC, roughly the period in which the birth of Jesus is thought to have occurred. There is, however, no evidence that associates a planetary conjunction such as this with a star.

Though these suggestions may appeal to some, there is no way to be sure that any of them is the correct explanation. The best we can do is to say that what the Magi saw was prepared by God so that these men from afar would come to pay homage to the Son of God.

These men who were representative of the outside world recognized the divine nature of this One who had recently been born. Their homage demonstrated that Jesus had come to be the Savior of the world, and not just of the Jews.

Herod's Response (Matthew 2:3-8)

Herod had spent most of his life either fighting to get his throne or struggling to hold on to it. He had not been born king of the Jews. He had seized the throne by intrigue, murder, and raw power. Nothing disturbed him more than the fear that someone with a rightful claim would take the kingdom from him. During his latter years nearly all of Herod's energies were directed against those who might be trying to steal his throne from him. Therefore, when these eastern visitors announced that they had come seeking one who had recently been born and was king by right of birth, Herod was troubled.

Matthew was not guilty of exaggeration here. When King Herod was troubled, so was everyone else. In fits of rage, he had executed so many people that no one was sure whose head might be next. Therefore when the people of Jerusalem heard that Herod was troubled, they became troubled also.

The request of the Wise Men was one that Herod was not equipped to handle alone. He was no expert on the Hebrew Scriptures. So he called the religious leaders of the Jews and asked them about the birthplace of the Messiah. He called together the chief priests as well as the scribes. During the interbiblical period, the high priesthood of the Jews had been corrupted. During the first century, several high priests were living at once. This would have been true during this stage of Herod's life. The living ex-high priests along with other ruling priests made up the body of religious rulers. The scribes were the Old Testament scholars as well as scholars of the oral law. So Herod summoned the religious hierarchy of the Jews as well as their biblical experts. To them he put the question of the birthplace of the Christ.

There was no hesitation on their part. They were well versed in the Old Testament, and they knew immediately the answer to Herod's question.

They did not leave Herod wondering long as to the source of their answer. They knew exactly where their answer had come from. Their source was Micah 5:2. The form of verb "it is written" is the regular formula used in the New Testament for citing an Old Testament statement. It could well be paraphrased "it is on record." As far as they were concerned, there was no room for debate on the matter. The prophet Micah had written that the Christ was to be born in Bethlehem.

Bethlehem was a small and in some respects insignificant village. However, Bethlehem had its own claim to fame, for Bethlehem had been David's hometown. The reference to the town as being among the "rulers of Judah" (RSV) is probably an allusion to the fact that this was David's home.

The term *ruler* could well be translated "leader" or "prince." Bethlehem was not only David's town, it also was to be the Messiah's place of birth. From this small town, the perfect prince of Israel was to come forth.

The word translated "govern" (NASV) literally means to shepherd. The shepherd led his sheep and cared for them. He also provided pasture for them by day and protection for them by night. So the Messiah will lead, make provisions for, and protect his people.

Now that Herod had the information he wanted from the Jewish religious leaders, he was through with them. They were no longer necessary to his plans. So he secretly summoned the Wise Men to his presence.

A star appearing in the heavens to represent a great person was supposed to appear on the day of his birth. Herod was trying to determine the age of this infant who was a possible threat to his throne.

Though we have no sure way of determining just what the Wise Men told Herod concerning the date of the star's appearance, it is worth noting that when Herod saw that his plans were foiled, he killed the infants two years old and under (v. 16). This is one reason why students of the New Testament conclude that the Wise Men did not visit the Christ child on the night of his birth, as did the shepherds. Their visit probably occurred some months after his birth. This of course should help us to see that the true spirit of Christmas should be a part of the Christian's total life perspective. It should not be experienced for just a few short days of every year.

After Herod had found the information desired by the Wise Men, he dispatched them on their way to Bethlehem.

As Herod gave them these instructions, he was showing remarkable constraint, concealing the jealousy that was raging within his soul. He was able to hide his hatred long enough to fool them.

Herod knew the intent of the Wise Men, and he pretended that he also had a desire to pay homage to the Christ child. Therefore, he instructed them to bring him word of his whereabouts.

Had the Wise Men known anything at all about the character of King Herod, they surely would not have trusted him as they did. Herod was able to contain his jealous rage long enough to deceive the visitors. He fooled them into thinking that he also desired to worship the infant King. He instructed them to go to Bethlehem and find the Christ child and then bring him word. Thus these well-meaning men were being used as pawns in a deadly and sinister plot against the newborn King.

The Wise Men in Bethlehem (Matthew 2:9-12)

Whether or not the star had given them direction all along on their journey this far is not clear. The language, however, seems to indicate that up to this point it had not. Surely the star had not led them to Herod's palace. Matthew appears to be saying that the star had appeared first when Jesus was born. Now it reappeared to direct them to Bethlehem. The tense of the verb indicates that the star was moving to the resting place of the Christ child.

Not only did the star direct them to the village; it directed them to the very place where the Christ child was. It stopped over the area, if not the very house, and seemed to point to the infant King.

The Wise Men were very happy to see the star again and to have it give direction to their journey. Perhaps this is suggestive of the universal nature of Christianity. These Gentiles were given divine direction to the exact place where the incarnate Son of God lay as an infant. God himself was opening the door for the world outside Judaism to come and pay homage to his Son.

The word used here for "house" is that of a permanent dwelling. They were no longer in the stable near the inn. No mention is made here of a manger or swaddling clothes. This visit apparently was several months after his birth. Joseph and Mary now seemed to be making Bethlehem their home.

Luke 2:21 tells of Jesus being taken to the Temple for circumcision when he was eight days old. Luke 2:22 tells of another visit to the Temple for Mary's ceremony of purification after childbirth. The Law prescribed that this be done forty days after childbirth (Lev. 12:1-4). The visits to the Temple recorded in Luke 2:21-38 must have taken place before the Wise Men came. Joseph would not have risked a visit to Jerusalem after the warning recorded in Matthew 2:13.

Luke 2:21-22 also helps explain why Mary and Joseph had remained so long in Bethlehem. Apparently they wanted to remain until they had completed their religious duties in Jerusalem. Nazareth was many miles from Jerusalem, but Bethlehem was only a few miles away.

The fact that Matthew did not mention Joseph should be regarded as merely incidental. It is simply a natural thing to associate a young child with his mother.

The Wise Men had come to their journey's end. The object of their search was before them. Recognizing his importance, they fell down and worshiped him. They bowed before him in recognition of the fact that he was born to be King. Here the outside world is admitted to the presence of the Christ and worships him as King.

It is still a custom in some parts of the world that when one visits royalty, he brings a gift to the king. The oriental custom of bearing gifts when one visits someone of superior rank or station in life is also a part of what is seen here. The Wise Men looked upon him as royalty, and as such they were prepared to offer him their gifts.

Over the years, tradition has added to the simple facts of this episode. Matthew tells us only that some Wise Men brought three gifts—gold, frankincense, and myrrh. Tradition has interpreted this to mean that three Wise Men came. Later tradition even assigned a name and a distinctive description to each Wise Man. According to tradition, one was old, one was middle-aged, and one was young. Tradition even assigned symbolic meanings to each of the gifts. Gold was for Jesus' royalty; frankincense was for his deity; and myrrh was for his burial. We need to distinguish between what the biblical record states and what tradition has added.

What form of warning they received in the dream is of little importance. They were, at any rate, diverted from their determined course.

Divine intervention is seen here. Herod's sinister plot to use them was thwarted. He was not able to use the Wise Men any further for his own selfish purposes.

The Flight to Egypt (Matthew 2:13-15)

Though Matthew does not say how long the Wise Men had been gone, the indication seems to be that this occurred soon after their departure.

This was not the first time Joseph had received a heavenly visitor in a dream. The importance of the message to Joseph is hereby emphasized.

The border of Egypt was less than one hundred miles

from Bethlehem. At this time in history, Egypt was a Roman province; however, it was well outside the jurisdiction of Herod. A large Jewish community lived within the major cities of Egypt, so Joseph and Mary would have been well received in almost any part of the country. They were told to go there and stay until they received further orders.

The reason for the flight was explained to Joseph. Herod's insane jealousy knew no bounds. He would be enraged when he learned that the Wise Men had thwarted his plans. He would seek to destroy Jesus by devious methods. Therefore, they were to flee beyond his reach.

Being a devout man, Joseph accepted the message of the dream. When he awoke from his sleep, he gathered his belongings together, and he and Mary and Jesus headed toward Egypt.

Their stay in Egypt probably was not long in duration. Herod probably did not live more than a year or two after the birth of Jesus.

Matthew again reached into the Old Testament for a text concerning the Messiah. This time he used a statement from Hosea 11:1. In its context, the statement is a reference to Israel. Matthew may be saying that this instance in the life of Jesus is parallel to that incident in the life of Israel.

Verses 16-18 record the furious rage of Herod when he discovered that the Wise Men had frustrated his attempt to isolate the Christ child. Because of this, he slaughtered all of the babies two years old and under in Bethlehem. This act shows the deranged state of Herod's mind at this point in his life.

Verses 19-23 tell what happened when Herod died. An angel appeared in a dream to Joseph while he was in Egypt and instructed him to return to Israel with his family. Rather than return to Bethlehem, he went to Nazareth because he heard that Herod's son Archelaus was ruling in Judea. Archelaus had a reputation for being like his father. In Herod's will, Archelaus received Judea, the area where Bethlehem was, but not Galilee, where Nazareth was.

Matthew 2 is important in seeking to determine the year of Jesus' birth. In Jesus' day, dates were figured from the time of the founding of Rome. Several centuries after the time of Christ, a Christian named Dionysius Exiguus revised the system of dating. He used the birth of Jesus as the focal point. Dionysius correctly saw the coming of Christ as the midpoint of human history. However, he miscalculated by a few years. He dated Jesus' birth in the year 754 by the Roman system of dating. However, Herod died in 750, or 4 BC. We know from Matthew 2 that Jesus was born prior to Herod's death, but probably no more than two years before. Thus he was probably born somewhere between 6-4 BC. The exact year is not so important as a correct understanding of the significance of Jesus' birth.

Conclusion

Every season of the year is a proper time to respond positively to Jesus.—Though the coming of the Wise Men did not occur on the night of Jesus' birth, they are still very much a part of the Christmas story. Their coming should alert us to the fact that the celebration of Christ's coming should not be confined to one day or one season of the year. Every season of the year is a proper time for people to respond to Christ as the Wise Men did.

Some people respond negatively to Jesus.—There are two kinds of responses to Christ reflected in Matthew 2.

Herod's response of jealousy and rejection was based on fear that this infant might have a better claim to his throne than he did. People reject Jesus today for many reasons. The basic reason for rejecting him is always the same—the unwillingness to enthrone Christ in our lives.

Some respond positively to Jesus.—The Wise Men represent those who respond positively to Christ's coming. They were open and eager to receive revelations about Christ. When they found him they worshiped him, offering him gifts. Their response to Christ symbolized the eventual harvest of believers from all nations who respond positively to Christ's coming.

Some respond to Jesus by doing nothing.—Few people today are so violent in their rejection as Herod was. However, many people are like the chief priests and scribes. These people knew where the Messiah was to be born. Apparently, they knew why Herod wanted to know. However, they did not join the Wise Men in their pilgrimage to Bethlehem. Whether they acted out of fear or indifference we do not know; however, we know they did nothing. Many today know many of the facts about Jesus Christ. However, they are not interested enough to react positively or negatively. Indifference, of course, is only another form of rejection.

5
Rejoicing in the Incarnation

1 Now it came about in those days that a decree went out from Caesar Augustus, that a census should be taken of all the inhabited earth.

2 This was the first census taken while Quirinius was governor of Syria.

3 And all were proceeding to register for the census, everyone to his own city.

4 And Joseph also went up from Galilee, from the city of Nazareth, to Judea, to the city of David, which is called Bethlehem, because he was of the house and family of David,

5 in order to register, along with Mary, who was engaged to him, and was with child.

6 And it came about that while they were there, the days were completed for her to give birth.

7 And she gave birth to her firstborn son; and she wrapped Him in cloths, and laid Him in a manger, because there was no room for them in the inn.

8 And in the same region there were some shepherds staying out in the fields, and keeping watch over their flock by night.

9 And an angel of the Lord suddenly stood before them, and the glory of the Lord shone around them; and they were terribly frightened.

10 And the angel said to them, "Do not be afraid; for

behold, I bring you good news of a great joy which shall
be for all the people;

11 for today in the city of David there has been born for
you a Savior, who is Christ the Lord.

12 "And this will be a sign for you: you will find a baby
wrapped in cloths, and lying in a manger."

13 And suddenly there appeared with the angel a multitude of the heavenly host praising God, and saying,

14 "Glory to God in the highest,
And on earth peace among men with whom He is
pleased."

15 And it came about when the angels had gone away
from them into heaven, that the shepherds began saying
to one another, "Let us go straight to Bethlehem then,
and see this thing that has happened which the Lord has
made known to us."

16 And they came in haste and found their way to Mary
and Joseph, and the baby as He lay in the manger.

17 And when they had seen this, they made known the
statement which had been told them about this Child.

18 And all who heard it wondered at the things which
were told them by the shepherds.

19 But Mary treasured up all these things, pondering
them in her heart.

20 And the shepherds went back, glorifying and praising
God for all that they had heard and seen, just as had been
told them.

(Luke 2:1-20, NASB)

In these verses, Luke focuses attention on certain events
that surrounded the birth of Jesus. These wondrous events
that took place in Judea many years ago may have become
seemingly commonplace to us today, for we have heard of

them since childhood days. In fact, we have heard them so often that the message may have lost its wonder. As you read Luke 2:1-20, notice the recurrence of words that express joy, awe, and praise.

This passage is not just a recounting of ordinary historical facts. Here is a record of the time when the sovereign, immortal, invisible, eternal God invaded the realm of human history in a unique way. On that night long ago, heaven touched earth in a way that is unique and beautiful. Luke's Gospel shows us both the earthly and the heavenly aspects of that marvelous night. The birth of Jesus was a pivotal point in salvation history. At that point in time God took upon himself the limitations of flesh.

The Enrollment (Luke 2:1-5)

As was Luke's custom, he set the Gospel story within the historical framework of the world of the first century. That world was the Roman Empire in all of its pomp and grandeur. Augustus Caesar, known earlier as Octavius, ruled the Roman Empire from 30 BC until AD 14. He ruled over an empire that encompassed nearly all of the civilized world; thus a taxation decree from Augustus included faraway Judea.

Quirinius was the governor of Syria at this time. Galilee and Judea were ruled over by Herod (Matt. 2:1), but Herod ruled in the name of and by the permission of Rome. The Jews were under the general jurisdiction of the Roman governor of Syria. Luke's purpose in verses 1-2 was to help set the birth of Jesus Christ within the context of history. This is not a myth or fairy tale. It happened at a certain place in human history.

Verse 3 is a simple historical statement concerning the response of the people of Palestine to the decree of

Augustus. Augustus, like many Roman rulers, was wise enough to give some consideration to the national customs of his subject people. The going of each person to his ancestral city seems to have been a Jewish custom. Probably Augustus issued the general order and allowed Herod to administer it as he saw fit.

Joseph and Mary were living in Nazareth, a village nestled in the hills not far from the Sea of Galilee. However, Joseph was a descendant of David. Therefore, he journeyed south to Judea and to Bethlehem which was David's ancestral home (1 Sam. 17:12). Micah 5:2 contains a prophecy that the Messiah would be born in Bethlehem. Mary is referred to as Joseph's "betrothed." That is, the marriage had not yet been physically consummated. Matthew 1:24 tells us that Joseph married Mary soon after the announcement to him of Jesus' impending birth. Matthew 1:25 carefully emphasizes that although Joseph took her as his wife, the marriage was not physically consummated until after the birth of Jesus.

Did Mary go because women as well as men were required by law to be enrolled for taxation? Perhaps so. However, she may have gone along because Joseph wanted to be close at hand when the promised child was born. Possibly both were aware of Micah's prophecy about the Messiah's birth in Bethlehem. Whether they knew of this or not, we cannot say. However, viewing these events from a distance, we can see how such a thing as a taxation decree providentially set the stage for the birth of the promised Messiah in the city of David.

The Birth of Jesus (Luke 2:6-7)

In these two verses, Luke recorded one of the most marvelous events in salvation history. The birth of Jesus occurred like any other birth as far as outward appearances were concerned. But, in this event, the eternal, sovereign God invaded the world of men. The incarnation occurred, and Luke was able to record the event in the brief words of a simple narrative.

Luke does not tell us how long they were there before the child was born. The stay was not intended to be for very long, for they sought lodging in an inn. In the providence of God, the Christ child was not delivered before they reached the inn in Bethlehem.

In the language of a simple narrative, Luke recorded this glorious event. The reference to her "firstborn" son implies that she bore other children. The Gospels refer to brothers and sisters of Jesus (Mark 6:3). Presumably, these were children of Mary and Joseph.

Swaddling cloths were narrow strips of cloth that were wrapped around infants for the purpose of restricting their movements. Mary followed the custom of her day in caring for her firstborn.

Perhaps the birth took place in a cave near the inn or even connected with it in some way. The beasts of burden may have been quartered here, but the domestic animals probably were out in the fields. Whether or not the animals had recently been feeding in this particular manger cannot be ascertained, but some were probably near.

Many people had come to the village of Bethlehem because of the census; therefore, Mary and Joseph could find no place to lodge in the usual guest accommodations. Because of this, they had to lodge in the place where the beasts of burden would normally be quartered.

Thus in verses 6-7, Luke recorded for us with simplicity both the beauty and the pathos surrounding the birth of the Savior. As there was no place for him to be born in the inn, so many people throughout the years have had no place in their hearts for the Son of God.

Angels and Shepherds (Luke 2:8-14)

Verses 8-14 provide a beautiful centerpiece for Luke's narrative concerning the birth of the Lord Christ. Simple hill-folk were out with their flocks on a beautiful star-filled night, and suddenly all of heaven broke forth with the birth announcement of the Savior of the world. This took place in the area around Bethlehem, which is situated a few miles south of Jerusalem in the heart of the Judean hill country.

The date of our Savior's birth cannot be exactly determined. However, the time was very likely not during the month of December. The shepherds did not go into the fields with their flocks during the colder months. When Jesus was born, the weather was mild enough for them to be in the fields. The day and month chosen to celebrate our Lord's birth is of less significance than the manner in which his birth is celebrated.

The language used to describe the action of the shepherds may indicate that they were watching in turns. They had made camp in the area, and each of the shepherds in his turn was watching the flock. During this time, the angel stood by their side. Without any announcement or fanfare, the angel just stepped onto the scene. The darkness was dispelled by the glory of the Lord, and they were presently in the midst of the divine light.

Literally, "they feared with a great fear." They were in the midst of a most unusual experience. It was only normal that they should quake with fear. The angel's first words to the shepherds were a message of assurance; they did not need to fear. In the original, "be not afraid" is a strong negative prohibition, and may be rendered "stop being afraid." The angel had not come to cause them to fear but to bring a message that would put joy in their hearts. The word *good news* is the one translated *gospel* in many other contexts. On this beautiful starlit night on a lonely hillside in Judea, the first gospel pronouncement was made by an angel to a band of humble shepherds.

Though the shepherds were the first to hear the gospel announcement, it would not end with them. From the very beginning, the gospel has had universal implications. It was not to be captured and kept in Judea, but it was to be loosed and sent out to all people everywhere. The very fact that a group of humble shepherds were the first to hear was a clear indication that the message was not exclusive.

Though the details of the birth were not announced to the shepherds, they were clearly told the unique mission of the child born that night. He was to be the Savior. The angel's announcement to the shepherds is reminiscent of the angelic announcement to Joseph in Matthew 1:21 (RSV): "'She will bear a son, and you shall call his name Jesus, for he will save his people from their sins.'"

This particular combination of words (Savior, Christ the Lord) in reference to Jesus is found nowhere else in all of the New Testament. The term *Christ* is the Greek equivalent of the Hebrew *Messiah,* and it means an anointed one. In ancient times, kings were inaugurated by anointing. The Messiah was the promised King of David's line. This One who was born in unusual circumstances was the Jewish Messiah of promise. Beyond that, he was Lord in every sense of the word.

The angel expected the shepherds to go to Bethlehem to seek out the newborn Savior, so he gave them their directions. He told them what to look for when they arrived in the village of Bethlehem.

After the angel made the birth announcement, the whole

heavens burst forth with angelic presence. The word for *host* is a military word that was used for a band of soldiers. Here the heavenly army was on a different kind of mission. They had come to join in the birth announcement for the Christ child, the incarnate Deity.

The form of the verb *praising* indicates that they were doing so continually. What a wonderful way to celebrate the birth of the Savior of the world! Surely, as we celebrate the birth of the Lord Christ, our hearts should be filled with praise to God for his unspeakable gift.

The form of their praise is here indicated. They gave glory to the sovereign God. He had sent his Son to earth to dwell among men and be their Savior. Because of this the angelic choir raised their voices in praise to God.

The angelic choir sang praises of glory to God in heaven. They also announced that peace was to be the ultimate result of the Savior's coming. In some old copies of Luke, the word translated *good will* is listed along with *peace* as dual gifts from God to men. The oldest and best copies of Luke make "peace" the gift and "good will" as in some way related to the word "men." The meaning of this latter translation is not that God has in some way restricted his peace only to certain people. The angel had announced that the gift of joy was intended for all people (v.10). The same thing was surely true of the gift of peace. The point of verse 14 is that peace is a gift of God's grace to men. A better translation of the last part of verse 14 may be "and on earth peace among men, who are the objects (or recipients) of God's good pleasure (or grace)."

There can be no true peace among men until we are at peace with God. This is a part of the Christmas message that is often overlooked amid the glittering tinsel and blinking lights of this festive season. Christ came so that men might know the true peace that passes all understanding. As we rejoice in the coming of the Christ child during this Christmas season, let us seek to bring our celebration into a proper perspective.

Thus, verses 8 through 14 highlight one of the most beautiful parts of the Christmas story. Scarcely anything about the Christmas narrative excites our imagination more than the appearance of the angelic host to a humble band of shepherds in the lonely Judean hill country. The ways of God are sometimes strange to us. Why did God decide to announce Messiah's birth to these lowly hill-folk rather than to those in the palace or among the leading Pharisees of the land? Whatever his reasons, this beautiful pastoral scene leaves us all wondering with amazement.

To Bethlehem and Back (Luke 2:15-20)

Evidently the angels left the shepherds as suddenly as they had appeared to them.

Undoubtedly, the place where the shepherds were watching their flocks was not far from Bethlehem. Once they realized the import of the angelic announcement, they determined to go to Bethlehem and see the baby for themselves. They did not lose any time in making this journey to Bethlehem. They were anxious to see the baby who was to be the Savior of the world. Though Bethlehem was crowded due to the census, the village was quite small. Finding information about a woman who had given birth that night probably was not hard to do. There probably were not many births that particular night in Bethlehem. Surely there would not have been many others under the same circumstances as this one.

When they found Mary and Joseph, the shepherds reported what the angel had told them concerning Jesus and how the angelic choir had sung praises to God because of his birth. Luke 2:17 shows that the shepherds told not only Mary and Joseph but also others whom they met. Thus the shepherds became not only the first to hear the gospel but also the first to tell it. Those who heard the shepherds' story wondered at what they heard. Mary had very little to say about the whole episode. Rather, she began to think on all that had happened to her in the past months. She kept all of these things in her heart, and surely she wondered at what the future held for her firstborn Son.

After finding the babe just as the angel said they would, the shepherds returned to their camp. These humble Judean shepherds had been treated to a revelation from God. They had looked upon the miracle of the incarnation, and now they returned rejoicing.

This ought to be the keynote of our celebration of Christmas. We should rejoice because of what we have heard and seen in Jesus Christ. Because he has come, we have salvation and eternal life. Our hearts should sing with praise as we approach the celebration of his birth.

Conclusion

This passage is Luke's record of the night of Jesus' birth. If we are not careful, we will skim over it too quickly and superficially because of our familiarity with it. Our study of the passage ought to catch us up in the wonder and praise of the shepherds and the angelic host.

The story of Christ's coming is real.—It is salvation history, but it is real history. On that night so long ago, heaven touched earth in the most unusual way. As Luke recounts the incidents, he reflects on both the human side and the divine side. He shows us both the wonder of the shepherds and the glorious praise of the angelic chorus. In studying this passage, we must not lose sight of the fact that we are dealing with history. This is no make-believe fairy tale. Luke was recording salvation history for mankind.

The message of Christ's birth is good news.—The angel's announcement and the angelic song are concise summaries of the best news the world has ever heard. The child born in Bethlehem's manger was the fulfillment of God's careful planning and of mankind's ageless yearnings. The child was the Savior of the world, Christ, the Lord. He came as an expression of God's grace to mankind. He came bringing a message of joy and peace to all people.

This message was meant to be believed and to be told. The shepherds believed; they went and saw for themselves; and they told others what they had seen and heard. How tragic it would have been if they had not gone to Bethlehem and seen for themselves! Equally tragic would have been their failure to tell others what they had seen and heard. The full joy of Christ's coming was theirs because they listened, believed, obeyed, experienced, told, and worshiped. Their response on that first night is a model for all of us in later years who would respond properly to the good news of Christ's coming.

PART II

Meditations on the Incarnation

6
Be Born in
Us Today

11 You will be enriched in everything for all liberality, which through us is producing thanksgiving to God.
12 For the ministry of this service is not only fully supplying the needs of the saints, but is also overflowing through many thanksgivings to God.
13 Because of the proof given by this ministry they will glorify God for your obedience to your confession of the gospel of Christ, and for the liberality of your contribution to them and to all,
14 while they also, by prayer on your behalf, yearn for you because of the surpassing grace of God in you.
15 Thanks be to God for His indescribable gift!

(2 Corinthians 9:11-15, NASB)

In a rustic cave just outside the sleepy little village of Bethlehem almost two thousand years ago, an event occurred which has forever changed the face of history. A young woman gave birth to a man-child and laid him in a manger where animals were fed. Today that spot is marked by the magnificent structure called the Church of the Nativity. No one knows for sure that this is the exact spot, but the church was built over a cave purported to be the birthplace of the Christ child. This church was first erected here in the fourth century by the emperor Constantine at the traditional place of Jesus' birth. If one can overlook the ceremonial trappings of many centuries, a genuine experience of worship can be had in this place. To stand at the entrance to the grotto or cave and pray that the Christ of Christmas be born in us anew can be a marvelous experience indeed. Each time I have stood in this place on my several pilgrimages to the Holy Land I have been moved to worship the babe of Christmas who is now my risen, living Lord, and I have felt like singing the carol:

O little town of Bethlehem,
How still we see thee lie!
Above thy deep and dreamless sleep
The silent stars go by;
Yet in thy dark streets shineth
The everlasting Light;
The hopes and fears of all the years
Are met in thee tonight.

For Christ is born of Mary,
And gathered all above,
While mortals sleep, the angels keep
Their watch of wond'ring love.
O morning stars, together
Proclaim the holy birth,
And praises sing to God the King,
And peace to men on earth!

How silently, how silently
The wondrous gift is giv'n!
So God imparts to human hearts
The blessings of his heav'n.
No ear may hear his coming,
But in this world of sin,
Where meek souls will receive him, still
The dear Christ enters in.

O holy child of Bethlehem!
Descend to us, we pray;
Cast out our sin, and enter in,
Be born in us today!
We hear the Christmas angels
The great glad tidings tell;
O come to us, abide with us,
Our Lord Immanuel!
(Phillips Brooks)

In what way can the Christ of Christmas be born in us? How in heaven's name can such a thing as this take place? To be sure, it is a mystical concept which does not admit to an easy explanation in concrete terms. Webster's New Collegiate Dictionary defines the term *mystical* as "having a spiritual meaning or reality that is neither apparent to the senses nor obvious to the intelligence." However, just because we do not fully understand it or cannot explain it in concrete terminology, it is not any less real.

As we trust Christ for salvation, he comes to dwell in our hearts. By faith we open our hearts to him, and he is born in us anew. We speak of this event as a new birth or as salvation, and it is surely both of these. But in a very real sense the Christ of Christmas is born in us when we trust him as our Savior.

When Christ is born in us we become a part of his body corporate—the church. He is our head, and we are one of the members of his body. As such, we become extensions of the incarnation. Christ is living out his ministry through us. This is part and parcel of Paul's theology. Notice what he said in Galatians 2:20 (NASB): "I have been crucified with Christ; and it is no longer I who live, but Christ lives in me; and the *life* which I now live in the flesh I live by faith in the Son of God, who loved me, and delivered Himself up for me." Our mission in life as Christians is to show forth Christ to a lost and dying world. We can do this in many ways, but a primary way is to allow Christ to live out his ministry through us. This has nothing to do with how hard we try to be good persons. Rather this has to do with the surrender of our very beings to Christ. It has to do with allowing him to live through us. To the extent that we allow him to live through us and minister through us, we are to that extent an extension of the incarnation.

As we are born anew, and as we become extensions of the incarnation because the Christ of Christmas has been born in us, so we should share the joy of Christmas with others. There are so many around us who do not know the true joys of Christmas. For all too many in our culture, Christmas has become simply a time of profiteering without any understanding of the true joys of the season. For some, Christmas heralds a time of unrestrained indulgence in alcohol consumption with all of the woes that accompany such activity. Surely those of us in whom Christ has been born bear the responsibility as well as the privilege of sharing with those around us the true joys of this season. The joy of giving at this time of the year stems from the fact that God has given to us the greatest gift of all in the Christ of Christmas. There is also the joy of knowing him whom to know aright is life eternal. How sorely our world needs to hear the true message of Christmas! They can hear it only as we will allow Christ to live out his ministry through us as we become extensions of his incarnation.

7
Born a King

1 Now after Jesus was born in Bethlehem of Judea in the days of Herod the king, behold, magi from the east arrived in Jerusalem, saying,
2 "Where is He who has been born King of the Jews? For we saw His star in the east, and have come to worship Him."

(Matthew 2:1-2, NASB)

In the last stanza of his hymn "Come, Thou Long-Expected Jesus," Charles Wesley quite well expressed the idea that Christ was born a king:

> Born thy people to deliver,
> Born a child, and yet a King,
> Born to reign in us forever,
> Now thy gracious kingdom bring.

During the Christmas season, we celebrate the birth of One whom the Bible says was born a king. It is interesting to note that the Bible does not say that he was born *to be* a king. He was not destined to be a king. He was a king by right of birth—whether or not people recognize him. His kingship is not dependent upon human recognition. His kingship is of divine, rather than human, origin.

It is interesting also to note that the Bible does not say

that his was a royal birth. There is no hint that the outward circumstances of his birth would have caused anyone to proclaim him king. There was none of the royalty of earth in attendance at his birth. Instead, his birth, which took place in a cave where animals were kept and fed, was attended by lowly shepherds from the Judean hills who had witnessed the angelic announcement of his birth. Nothing of the pomp and ceremony that generally accompanies the birth of earth's royalty surrounded his birth. Rather, the outward circumstances of his birth were just the opposite of what one would expect of royalty.

Yet the Scripture says explicitly that he was born a king. Let us consider some of the aspects of his kingship as well as the implications of this kingship for our lives. This may appear to some to be a strange emphasis to give to the Christmas story, but these things are very much a part of the broader implications of our Lord's birth.

First, let us contrast the kingship of Christ with that of Herod the Great. Herod was not a Jew. He was an Idumaean, and because of this the Jews hated and mistrusted him. He had married a Maccabaean princess hoping that this would cause the Jews to accept his rule, but they only despised him more. He had established his rule through methodical acts of cruelty and cunning. His kingship was based on intrigue, murder, and relentless display of physical power. He allowed no person or group to stand in the way of his tyrannical rule.

At the time of Jesus' birth, Herod was a sickly old man who was insanely jealous, and he imagined that everyone was trying to dethrone him. Not too long before, he had imprisoned and put to death three of his sons. Sometime earlier in a jealous rage he had his favorite wife put to death. The Romans joked that it was safer to be Herod's pig than his son. For out of deference to his Jewish subjects he would not kill a pig. However, his sons were in mortal danger.

The strongest desire of Herod's heart was to be accepted by his Jewish subjects. However, because of his Idumaean ancestry they refused. They never allowed him to forget that he was not a Jew. The syntax of the passage indicates that the Magi spoke of Jesus as one who was king by right of birth. Herod probably began to imagine all sorts of things when he heard the Magi and their question. Was there possibly a member of the ruling Maccabaean family who had escaped his purge? Who was this infant claimant to his throne? He would do everything in his power to find this rival and kill him before the Jewish people found out about him.

Though Jesus was King by birth, his kingdom was not to consist of any physical realm. Years later, as Jesus spoke to Pilate, he said: "My kingdom is not of this world.. . . then would my servants fight" (John 18:36, NASB). Herod's kingdom was transient and temporal, but Jesus is an eternal King, and his realm is spiritual.

Jesus is King by birth because he was begotten by the Holy Spirit of God. Of God conceived and virgin born, he is our eternal King. Though his birth was his entrance into the world, it was not his beginning. It was only the vehicle by which the eternal became incarnate and manifested himself to men. His birth is unique in all of the annals of human history, and it sets him apart as the Son of God. Because of this he is our eternal King.

Furthermore, he is King by virtue of the fact that in his person resides true humanity and God of very God. In a perfectly integrated personality, he mediates God to man and represents man in the presence of God. Because of the incarnation, he can be called the Son of Man. His solidarity with humanity and all of our joys and sorrows is thus established. He is able to represent perfectly the needs of man in the presence of God because he was tempted in all points common to man yet without sin. He is Son of Man—Emmanuel—God with us. As the perfect representative of imperfect humanity, he is our King now and forever more.

As King he lays claim upon the lives of men and women everywhere. Whether or not we crown him as our King does not diminish his kingship in the least. He rules whether we allow him to rule in our lives or whether we refuse to allow him to rule in our lives. For some this may sound like a strange emphasis to place upon the Christmas story. During the Christmas season, we are prone to think of the baby Jesus. We even speak of bringing our gifts to him. However, the first thing he wants from us is our lives completely dedicated to him. Our material gifts in his name are hollow unless they are prompted by the true love of a dedicated life. Certainly the gifts we lay at his feet have their place in our worship of him. However, until we give ourselves to him, we really haven't given him anything at all.

He is our King, and because of this we owe him our allegiance. He desires and deserves more than the lip service which is given to him all too often. We must be willing for the Christ of Christmas to reign supremely in our hearts and lives.

As servants of the eternal King, obligation is laid upon us to make all people everywhere aware of his royal claim upon their lives. We are to witness to those around us of his saving power. We are to be willing to go abroad as missionaries if he calls us. If he does not call us to foreign lands, we are to be willing to undergird those who do go with our prayers and with our financial support.

Southern Baptists have said that it is our desire to confront every person in the world with the claims of Christ by the year 2000. We have the means at our disposal to do this, and we can do it if we will all become personally involved in this task of Bold Missions. We must be willing to give sacrificially and go to the ends of the earth if need be to carry the message of Christ to every person.

If we are to see Bold Mission Thrust become a reality, we must improve upon the record of past missionary involvement. In the less than 150 years of our denominational history, we have sent fewer than ten thousand foreign missionaries into the world. Of our more than 33,000 churches, fewer than 5,000 have supplied all of the foreign missionaries. Think of the impact upon our world if just one person from every one of our churches were to go as a foreign missionary. Surely our task is great, but it is not an impossible one. We have been called to serve the King of kings and to take the message of his love into all the world. Let's do it!

The words of the second stanza of Charles Wesley's hymn, "Come, Thou Long-Expected Jesus," express the spirit of this call to dedication:

> Born thy people to deliver,
> Born a child, and yet a King,
> Born to reign in us forever,
> Now thy gracious kingdom bring.
> By thine own eternal spirit
> Rule in all our hearts alone;
> By thine all-sufficient merit,
> Raise us to thy glorious throne.

8
Gifts for the King

1 Now after Jesus was born in Bethlehem of Judea in the days of Herod the king, behold, magi from the east arrived in Jerusalem, saying,

2 "Where is He who has been born King of the Jews? For we saw His star in the east, and have come to worship Him."

3 And when Herod the king heard it, he was troubled, and all Jerusalem with him.

4 And gathering together all the chief priests and scribes of the people, he *began* to inquire of them where the Christ was to be born.

5 And they said to him, "In Bethlehem of Judea, for so it has been written by the prophet,

6 'And you, Bethlehem, land of Judah;
Are by no means least among the leaders of Judah;
For out of you shall come forth a Ruler,
Who will shepherd My people Israel.'"

7 Then Herod secretly called the magi, and ascertained from them the time the star appeared.

8 And he sent them to Bethlehem, and said, "Go and make careful search for the Child; and when you have found Him, report to me, that I too may come and worship Him."

9 And having heard the king, they went their way; and lo, the star, which they had seen in the east, went on

before them, until it came and stood over where the Child was.

10 And when they saw the star, they rejoiced exceedingly with great joy.

11 And they came into the house and saw the Child with Mary His mother; and they fell down and worshiped Him; and opening their treasures they presented to Him gifts of gold and frankincense and myrrh.

12 And having been warned by God in a dream not to return to Herod, they departed for their own country by another way.

(Matthew 2:1-12, NASB)

This is one of the loveliest episodes connected with the birth of our Lord. Wise Men from the East came to Bethlehem bearing gifts for the newborn King. These Magi represented the remnants of the great Median Empire that challenged the Persians for leadership of the world during the time of David. Later they became more interested in spiritual and intellectual pursuits than in political power. They became to the Medo-Persian Empire what the Levites were to the nation of Israel. They believed that the heavens gave signs in the stars which portended both good and evil for all of mankind. These men combined a strange mixture of ancient science and the priestly arts in their religion. Kings from around the world sought them out to hear their words of wisdom as well as their prediction of things to come.

In the Gospel account, they are representative of the world outside of Judaism. Since they have come to pay homage to this newborn King, the implication is that he holds out hope to all of the world and not just to the nation of the Jews. Jesus was to break the narrow confines of national Judaism, and this is our first hint of this fact in the Gospel narrative.

When the Magi came to Jerusalem, they were not following the star. They had seen his star when they were in their homeland. That is, a new star had appeared in the heavens which presaged the birth of a new monarch. Among the nations of the ancient east, there was a widespread belief that a universal king would arise out of Judea. Having seen the new star and being aware of such a belief, these men hastened to Jerusalem, the Holy City of the Jews, in search of this newborn monarch. First they went to the temporal ruler of the land, Herod the Great. This was the natural thing for them to do, for one surely would expect to find the heir to the throne in the palace of the king. However, rather than the heir to the throne they found only confusion and intrigue in the palace of Herod. After they were apprised of the fact that Messiah was to be born in Bethlehem, the star once again enters the narrative. It stood over the house where Joseph and Mary had taken Jesus. The word which Matthew used for *house* in verse 11 is always used of a permanent dwelling. Therefore the visit of the Magi occurred sometime after the birth of Jesus. Probably the star had appeared in the heavens as much as two years prior to their visit. For according to Matthew 2:16 (NASV), Herod determined to kill the male children "from two years old and under, according to the time which he had ascertained from the Magi."

Many subsequent traditions concerning the Magi and their gifts have circulated through the various countries of Christendom. One early tradition about them claims that there were twelve of them. Undoubtedly, this tradition was influenced by the number of the disciples of our Lord. The strongest tradition today is that there were three of them. No doubt this tradition arose because of the number of gifts mentioned by Matthew. The truth is that we simply do not know how many there were. The later legends about the Magi have given names to them and have even contained descriptions of their physical appearance. The first of these Magi was Melchior, a very old man with white hair and a long beard who offered gold to our Lord. The second was Gaspar, who was young and beardless with a ruddy complexion, and he brought frankincense. The third was Balthasar, dark skinned and heavily bearded. His was the gift of myrrh.

From very early times Christians have also assigned special meanings for these gifts. Gold is the gift for a king. It was customary that no one should approach a king without a gift. Since gold was looked upon as the king of metals, it was considered to be a gift suited for a king. So the gift of gold was symbolic of his kingship.

Frankincense is the gift for Deity. It was used in the Temple rituals of sacrifice, and its pungent odor was thought to be pleasing to God. The odor of this spice filled the house of worship, so this gift was symbolic that Jesus is the Son of God.

Myrrh is a gift for one who is going to die. This substance was actually an embalming fluid. It was also used in anointing the body of a dead person. Thus the gift bore witness to the fact that Jesus came to die for the sins of mankind.

There also developed within the tradition of the Christian community a symbolism relating these gifts to different aspects of Christian response to Christ. Gold symbolized the virtue which should be a part of every believer's character. The character of the Christian ought to be as pure as gold that has been purged of all impurities by the refiner's fire. Frankincense symbolized prayer because of its association with worship. Since Jesus is the Son of God, he has made it possible for us to approach God in prayer. Therefore the Christian should be diligent in prayer. Myrrh was symbolic of the suffering which the Christian would be called upon to experience for the cause of Christ. If the world crucified our Savior, you can be sure it will seek to make it difficult for those who are his followers.

Though undoubtedly the names and descriptions of these Magi are legendary and the significance of the gifts a part of a lovely Christian tradition, they are nonetheless a most arresting part of the Christmas story. Jesus is the Son of God who came to die, and most certainly he is King of kings.

9
What's in a Genealogy?

1 The book of the genealogy of Jesus Christ, the son of David, the son of Abraham.

2 To Abraham was born Isaac; and to Isaac, Jacob; and to Jacob, Judah and his brothers;

3 and to Judah were born Perez and Zerah by Tamar; and to Perez was born Hezron; and to Hezron, Ram;

4 and to Ram was born Amminadab; and to Amminadab, Nahshon; and to Nahshon, Salmon;

5 and to Salmon was born Boaz by Rahab; and to Boaz was born Obed by Ruth; and to Obed, Jesse;

6 and to Jesse was born David the King.

And to David was born Solomon by her who had been the wife of Uriah;

7 and to Solomon was born Rehoboam; and to Rehoboam, Abijah; and to Abijah, Asa;

8 and to Asa was born Jehoshaphat; and to Jehoshaphat, Joram; and to Joram, Uzziah;

9 and to Uzziah was born Jotham; and to Jotham, Ahaz; and to Ahaz, Hezekiah;

10 and to Hezekiah was born Manasseh; and to Manasseh, Amon; and to Amon, Josiah;

11 and to Josiah were born Jeconiah and his brothers, at the time of the deportation to Babylon.

12 And after the deportation to Babylon, to Jeconiah was born Shealtiel; and to Shealtiel, Zerubbabel;

13 and to Zerubbabel was born Abiud; and to Abiud, Eliakim; and to Eliakim, Azor;
14 and to Azor was born Zadok; and to Zadok, Achim; and to Achim, Eliud;
15 and to Eliud was born Eleazar; and to Eleazar, Matthan; and to Matthan, Jacob;
16 and to Jacob was born Joseph the husband of Mary, by whom was born Jesus, who is called Christ.
17 Therefore all the generations from Abraham to David are fourteen generations; and from David to the deportation to Babylon fourteen generations; and from the deportation to Babylon to the time of Christ fourteen generations.

(Matthew 1:1-17, NASB)

There are few things in the Bible that are less meaningful to the modern reader than the many genealogies. Few moderns have much interest in lists of descendants and ancestors. People who read the Bible through will do mental gymnastics when they come to 1 Chronicles 1-9. Sometimes these biblical name lists have been used as the subject for risqué humor. For instance, in *Finian's Rainbow* it is said that once Adam and Eve ate from the apple tree, "they began the begat."

Certainly, we would not begin a book or a story with a list. One of the primary tenets of journalism is to capture the attention of your reader in the first paragraph. A genealogical table such as the one found in Matthew would surely "turn off' most western readers right away. However, for the ancients and particularly for the Jews this was an eye-catching way to begin a book. In addition to interesting Jewish readers, a genealogy also served at least three purposes in ancient times. In his book *Old Testament Genealogies,* R. R. Wilson states that there were three areas of social life served by oral genealogies. In the domestic area, a genealogy proved family as well as economic relationships. As a political document, it gave support for a line of heredity officeholders. The genealogy served a religious purpose, supporting the claim for a cultic office such as a priest. So the genealogy in ancient times not only established identity but also served to undergird status.

When Herod the Great was in power, he attempted to have all of the public genealogies burned so that no one among his Jewish subjects could prove a purer genealogy than his. From this we can see how important these documents were to the ancients.

The construction of Jesus' genealogy by Matthew is quite interesting. Most probably, the genealogy was structured as an aid to memory. In fact, much of Matthew's gospel account is structured in such a way as to aid the memory. The genealogy of our Lord was also arranged in such a way that the three divisions have fourteen generations each. The letters of the Hebrew alphabet had numeric equivalents. The alphabet of the Hebrews consisted only of consonants called radicals. The English equivalent for the three consonants in David's name are DVD. The letter D was assigned the numeric value of 4, and the letter V was assigned the numeric value of 6. The letters DVD added together equal 14, or the number of generations in each division of the genealogy. Thus Matthew was stressing the fact that Jesus was the Son of David.

By arranging the genealogy in this way some of the names were passed over. This fact did not concern the Jewish reader and should not concern us. The point

Matthew was making is that Jesus is the son of Abraham and the son of David. In his massive volume *The Birth of the Messiah,* Raymond Brown reminds us that

> only rather rarely and to a limited depth do ancient Semitic genealogies afford us a list of strictly biological ancestry—a factor that does not necessarily make them inaccurate since the intention of those who preserved them was not strictly biological. Too often the genealogies of Jesus have been read with the same expectations with which one reads the list of grandparents and great-grandparents constituting the frontispiece of the family Bible.[1]

There are several wonderful lessons to be learned from the genealogy of Jesus. As we approach the first words of the Gospel of Matthew, we find a subtle similarity to Genesis 5. In the opening words of Genesis 5, we read: "This is the book of the generations of Adam." In the Greek version of the Old Testament called the Septuagint, almost the exact wording is found that occurs in the Greek text of Matthew. In Genesis 5, the genealogy is that of Adam and of his descendants. In Matthew, the record is that of the ancestors of Jesus. In salvation history, Jesus is the second Adam, but there can be no genealogy of his descendants, for salvation history reached its goal in Jesus. He has come as true man, the second Adam, to establish a new line of spiritual descendants—who cannot be named because of the number.

The three stages in this genealogy are representative of three stages in the history of the Hebrew nation. The first is that stage which occurred from Abraham to David and represents two of the zeniths in Hebrew history. Abraham was the progenitor of the Jewish race and as such was looked upon as the apex of human achievement. As far as the Jews were concerned, Abraham was the finest human being who had ever lived. Truly he represented one of the zeniths of their race.

Much occurred in the history of the Jewish nation between Abraham and David. There were highs and lows, good times and bad times. There were the years of bondage in Egypt as well as the wilderness wanderings. Great leaders like Moses, Joshua, and Caleb emerged. The Promised Land was subdued and settled, and there was the period of the judges before the emergence of the monarchy under Saul. The nation, however, did not reach its zenith until the time of David. During the reign of David, the nation realized much of the material and spiritual blessings God had promised to Abraham and to his seed. David was a great warrior statesman who led the Israelites during the time that they were a world power.

The Jews always thought of their nation as the recipient of the great promises of God. Historically, they saw these promises realized to some extent in the rule of David. However, all that David represented ideally was to find fruition in the Messiah, who was to be the ideal son of David. He would be David's ideal son not just in fleshly lineage, though this was true. He was to bring to fruition the promises of God to Abraham and to David. This is why Matthew stresses from the very first words in his Gospel that his is a record of the generations of Jesus Christ, Son of Abraham, Son of David.

The period of the genealogy from David to the captivity marked a time of decline and disintegration for the nation Israel. When Solomon died and his son Rehoboam became king, the dissolution of the united kingdom became a reality. Jeroboam, the son of Nebat, ascended to the throne in Samaria and immediately led the Northern Kingdom into the ways of idolatry. He was afraid that his subjects would be loyal to the national shrine at Jerusalem unless he set up shrines in his realm to compete. Thus he set up altars at Dan in the northern extremity and at Bethel in the southern extremity. He caused his people to worship the golden calf of Egypt. Because of their idolatry the Northern Kingdom was destroyed in 722 BC by Sargon II. The Southern Kingdom of Judah had its ups and downs, but the end result was inevitable. This was a shameful and sorrowful period in the genealogy. The bottom was finally reached when Jeconiah was led away captive with the princes of Judah.

The third phase of the genealogy represents an uphill climb from the depths at the time of the captivity to the lofty heights reached in Messiah. God reached down among the captives in Babylon and brought forth a remnant. From the many who went to Babylon captive the few were brought out in the remnant. This was a time of new beginnings under Ezra, Nehemiah, Zerubbabel and others. Now the Messiah has come in Jesus, Son of Abraham, Son of David. What Israel was ideally in David would be brought to actuality in Christ. David was a political deliverer, but Jesus was to be a spiritual savior.

Is not this genealogy also the story of mankind? Man was created for greatness. In the image of God man was created for fellowship with God. However, man through his own folly lost that for which he was created. He refused to acknowledge God as supreme in his life. He wanted to be the "whole cheese." He would be king and determine his own destiny. Because of this he went into the captivity to sin. Rather than be a friend of God, he became a slave to sin. Left to his own ways, man frustrated God's plan for him.

Though man abandoned God, he can find that destiny for which he was intended. God did not leave man to his own folly. God himself came in the flesh in the person of

Jesus, the Messiah, to condemn sin and redeem man. This is the true end of the book of the generations of Jesus, the Messiah: Man is rescued from his plight as a sinner and redeemed, so that he might realize his true destiny as a child of God.

Note

1. Raymond Brown, *The Birth of the Messiah* (New York: Doubleday, 1977), p. 65.

10
Who Was That Man?

27 And Jesus went out, along with His disciples, to the villages of Caesarea Philippi; and on the way He questioned His disciples, saying to them, "Who do people say that I am?"
28 And they told Him, saying, "John the Baptist; and others say Elijah; but still others, one of the prophets."
29 And He continued by questioning them, "But who do you say that I am?" Peter answered and said to Him, "Thou art the Christ."

(Mark 8:27-29, NASB)

The western hero in the legend of the Lone Ranger never revealed his identity to those whom he helped. Generally after he had done a good deed he rode off into the sunset on his white horse. The question "Who was that masked man?" was generally asked in hushed tones, and someone would always reply, "That was the Lone Ranger."

The same question has been asked concerning Jesus through the years, and many answers have been given. Among his contemporaries, there was uncertainty as to his identity. Some said that he was John the Baptist come back from the dead. Of course, Jesus was connected with John in the beginning of his ministry, and their messages had some similarities. Others said that Jesus was Elijah redivivus. Jesus had said that John the Baptist was the coming Elijah; however, the general populace never connected the two. There was a rabbinic tradition that Elijah would come before Messiah, and some in the crowds mistook Jesus for the forerunner instead of the Messiah. Others said that Jesus was the prophet Jeremiah. Perhaps Jesus was mistaken for Jeremiah because he was much like him. As Jeremiah wept over the city of Jerusalem, so Jesus wept often for the people of his nation. Jeremiah was a compassionate person, and we know that the compassion of our Lord is unparalleled in all of the annals of history. But, Jesus was not Jeremiah, Elijah, or John the Baptist. Then just who was he? Peter answered: "The Christ of God" (Luke 9:20). He is God's Anointed One—the one appointed to bring God's kingdom among men.

When we answer the question "Who was Jesus?" we must do it personally and individually, for ourselves. No one else can answer this question for us. There are many ways that we can express our faith in him, but what we really think of his person is of extreme importance.

Christmas is a time of celebration, but it is also a season of confession. Just who is this One whose birthday we celebrate? What can we say about his person that will help us to make a meaningful confession of our faith? Many titles are used for Jesus in both the Old and New Testaments. Lord, Savior, Emmanuel, Righteous Branch, My Servant David, Root of Jesse, Wonderful Counselor are but a few of the names that have been used of him. Meditating on some of these titles may make it possible for us to make the confession of our faith more meaningful.

To be sure he is God Incarnate. In Jesus Christ, God has come to us. He is the enfleshment of the invisible, immortal, eternal God. He is the God-man. Now Jesus is all God, but he is not all of God. Jesus was aware of the God beyond him, and he prayed often to the Father. To say that one can rationally explain the process involved in the incarnation is sheer folly. This fact, however, does nothing to diminish its reality. The miracle of miracles is that the omniscient, omnipresent God could become incarnate. If there is one thing which the New Testament teaches and of which orthodox Christians have been sure throughout the centuries since his coming, it is that Jesus Christ is the incarnation of Deity. He is not half-God and half-man. He is not a third kind of being, neither fully God nor fully man. Rather he is fully God and fully man in one totally-integrated personality.

He is Emmanuel, God with us. John said in his account that the Word has tabernacled with us. God has come to us supremely, decisively, and ultimately in Jesus Christ. As our Emmanuel, he is with us in our conflicts. When problems arise, and it is difficult for us to find the proper solution, he is with us to direct us in our efforts and to lead us through the labyrinth of life.

When sorrows come to fill our days with travail and grief, there is One who is present with us to guide us to a brighter day. He is Emmanuel—God with us.

On other days, when life is a constant song and joy floods our soul, he also is there. For he does not depart no matter what the circumstance. He is with us to bless, encourage, strengthen, and confirm. There is not a circumstance in life in which he is not Emmanuel.

He also is our Savior. His name implies this for Jesus means "salvation is of the Lord." The angel said to Joseph: "And you shall call His name Jesus, for it is He who will save His people from their sins" (Matt. 1:21b, NASB). In ancient times a man's name was supposed to describe his character. If it didn't, the person usually was given a nickname which did describe his character. For instance,

James and John were called "sons of thunder" because of their volatile temperaments. So, when the angel gave instructions to Joseph concerning the name for the Christ, he was also alerting Joseph to the character that Jesus would display.

As our Savior, he brings us into a right relationship with God. This is accomplished through a personal encounter with him through faith. People do not arrive at a right relationship with God through keeping a set of laws or repeating a creedal confession. The only way one comes into this relationship is by a faith commitment to him who came to save us from our sins.

Christ is Lord as well as Savior. He is the exalted one who has commissioned us to tell the good news of salvation to all people everywhere. As Lord, he sends us forth with the message of Emmanuel and Savior. The story of Christmas begins with the babe in a manger, but it does not end there. The message of Christmas is the good news that our God has come to us and has brought us salvation. This wonderful season reminds us that God has given to us the greatest gift that we could ever imagine. Only those who have experienced the truth of Emmanuel and Savior can appreciate the true message of Christmas.

Who was that man? Son of Mary, Son of God, he is our Emmanuel, and because he has come, we can sing:

> O come, O come, Emmanuel
> And ransom captive Israel,
> That mourns in lonely exile here,
> Until the Son of God appear.
>
> O come, thou Dayspring, come and cheer
> Our spirits by thine advent here;
> Disperse the gloomy clouds of night,
> And death's dark shadows put to flight.

O come, thou Wisdom from on high,
And order all things, far and nigh;
To us the path of knowledge show,
And cause us in her ways to go.

O come, Desire of nations, bind
All peoples in one heart and mind,
Bid envy, strife, and quarrels cease;
Fill the whole world with heaven's peace.

(Latin text, translated by John Mason Neale
and Henry Sloane Coffin)

II
Why Christmas?

8 And in the same region there were some shepherds staying out in the fields, and keeping watch over their flock by night.

9 And an angel of the Lord suddenly stood before them, and the glory of the Lord shone around them; and they were terribly frightened.

10 And the angel said to them, "Do not be afraid; for behold, I bring you good news of a great joy which shall be for all the people;

11 for today in the city of David there has been born for you a Savior, who is Christ the Lord.

12 And this will be a sign for you: you will find a baby wrapped in cloths, and lying in a manger."

13 And suddenly there appeared with the angel a multitude of the heavenly host praising God, and saying,

14 "Glory to God in the highest,
  And on earth peace among men with whom He is
    pleased."

(Luke 2:8-14, NASB)

Why do we celebrate Christmas? What's the purpose of the season? What reason did God have for bringing all of this to pass? Surely we claim that Christmas is the time when we celebrate the birthday of the King of kings. But in what spirit do we celebrate his birth? Do we truly honor him whose birth we celebrate?

In the statement made by the angel to the shepherds and in the words of the angel chorus, the real purpose of Christmas is set forth for us. We are told in these words why God brought all of this about, why the sovereign God became a man.

The first reason God has come to us in Jesus Christ is to dispel fear from our hearts. The angel was speaking to the shepherds concerning their fear, but I believe that we can say that this is a word for all of us. Throughout the years of history man has had to face many fears. Fear of many things dogs us from the cradle to the grave. The child fears to be away from Mother and Daddy. Young people fear that they will not be accepted by their peers or that their parents will be displeased with them. Married people fear the deaths of their spouses, and workers are afraid of losing their jobs. Mankind has fought the fear of his environment as well as the works of nature. Now in our enlightened age, we must combat the fear created by the ingenuity of man. Anyway we look at it, fear has been one of man's main enemies throughout the centuries.

The message of the angel rings out loud and clear across the centuries, "Fear not!" Surely the coming of Christ ought to dispel fear from the hearts of those who trust him for salvation. However, the truth of the matter is that we must allow him to dispel our fear. His coming does not automatically and mechanically do away with our fears or those things which cause our fears. If we will allow him, he will give us power over our fears and anxieties. As the child who is afraid of the dark by himself can be calmed by the touch of his father's hand, so when we place our trust in Christ and his power to guard us, our fears will disappear.

When we claim fully the promises related to the incarnation we need not fear anyone or anything.

Another purpose of this wonderful event that we call Christmas is to bring good tidings of great joy to all people. Of course the good news is that God has sent his Son into the world, so that all who relate to him through faith might have salvation. We should note that there is a universal significance to the angel's declaration. The purpose of Christ's coming is to bring these good tidings to *all* people. This message is not to be the precious possession of a few select people. Rather this message is for all who will receive it. The rich, the poor, the educated, the Black man, the white man, the Oriental, and the Latin American are all precious in God's sight. We are not to hoard the Good News, but we are to share the Good News with everyone, everywhere.

In a very real sense, Jesus was the Messiah of the Jews, but just as surely he came to be a universal Savior. His coming is good news for every person in all the world. The expression *good tidings* is built on the same basic root from which the word *gospel* comes. The incarnation makes the gospel a reality. Without Christmas there could have been no Easter. So Christmas really is the foundation stone for the good news of the gospel. When a person is properly related to the Christ of Christmas, there will be great joy within that person's heart. The true joys of Christmas are for those who know and have experienced the true meaning of the season.

Until one is properly related to the Christ of Christmas, one cannot truly celebrate the season. That is why there are so many aberrations that parade under the guise of celebrations during the Christmas season. Amid all the signs of the commercialization of the season—the rhythmic tune of the computerized cash registers, the glitter of the tinsel and myriads of toys, the "Ho, Ho, Ho" of the department store Santas, the colored lights and colorful wreaths that decorate our city streets—amid all those things, one will find an occasional manger scene, a tip of the hat to the babe of Bethlehem in whose coming is discovered the real meaning of the season.

For many poor, misguided folk, Christmas means the festal merriment engendered by the spirits of fermented grapes or grain rather than the true spirit of the season fostered by the indwelling Spirit of the living God. This sort of activity is a mockery to the true meaning of this holy season.

Christmas should bring glory to God in the highest. Surely, in the most blessed of Christian seasons, we are to glorify the God who sent his Son into the world that we might have eternal life. We should bring glory to God by our words as well as by our actions. We can bring glory to God by demonstrating to the world the love of God. We must allow God to love the world through us, for how else will the world truly know of the love of God? Our words of love are of little value unless we prove by our actions that our love is real. When we show the world what God is like, we truly bring glory to him.

By sending his Son as our Savior, God has truly glorified himself. For, through this means, he has shown us the true nature of his eternal love. God's glory is his radiance and splendor reflected in his character. One of the oldest meanings of the Greek word translated "glory" is that of reputation. When one's reputation and character are the same and both are what they ought to be, then there is glory. When God sent his Son into the world, he established in concrete reality the fact that his reputation as well as his character consists of an unfettered, immeasurable love for creation. Jesus glorified the Father in his life as well as his death. His life was lived completely within the circle of his Father's will. When he went to the cross, he told his disciples that through his death the Father would be glorified in the Son. So truly the Christ of Christmas brings glory to God in the highest.

Christmas has yet another purpose and that is to bring peace among men in whom God is well pleased. If the glory of God in the highest is revealed in the coming of his Son, then the result for men on earth can be summed up by the word *peace*. More than the cessation of strife is meant by the word *peace* here. The word is used here to indicate all of the blessings of God that are in any way connected to the coming of his Son into the world. These are messianic blessings, if you will. He has come to bring a new situation of peace between God and men as well as between man and man.

The Christ of Christmas will bring peace to the hearts of all those who trust him. When we become properly related to him through faith, our hostility toward God ceases. Beyond that, the hostilities with our fellowmen are also eliminated. Our trust in Christ takes care of our vertical relationships as well as our horizontal relationships. This is the kind of total well-being which a simple trust in the Christ of Christmas will bring.

There is no automatic peace on earth and goodwill to men because of the coming of Christ. This never has been, nor can it ever be. However, through the coming of Christ, God has made a situation of peace obtainable. When people respond properly to the Christ of Christmas, there will be a genuine peace in their hearts, and they in turn can impart this peace to others. To the extent that we allow it to happen, God will give us peace.

12

Good News of Great Joy

1 Now it came about in those days that a decree went out from Caesar Augustus, that a census be taken of all the inhabited earth.

2 This was the first census taken while Quirinius was governor of Syria.

3 And all were proceeding to register for the census, everyone to his own city.

4 And Joseph also went up from Galilee, from the city of Nazareth, to Judea, to the city of David, which is called Bethlehem, because he was of the house and family of David;

5 in order to register, along with Mary, who was engaged to him, and was with child.

6 And it came about that while they were there, the days were completed for her to give birth.

7 And she gave birth to her firstborn son; and she wrapped Him in cloths, and laid Him in a manger, because there was no room for them in the inn.

8 And in the same region there were some shepherds staying out in the fields, and keeping watch over their flock by night.

9 And an angel of the Lord suddenly stood before them, and the glory of the Lord shone around them; and they were terribly frightened.

10 And the angel said to them, Do not be afraid; for

behold, I bring you good news of a great joy which shall be for all the people.

(Luke 2:1-10, NASB)

What is the best news you ever received? How did you react when you heard it? Did it produce excitement, or did it bring peace? Was there a feeling of exhilaration, or did a calm feeling settle over you? Perhaps you experienced something of all of these emotions and maybe even more than these.

I'm sure that those shepherds tending their sheep in the Judean hills near the sleepy little village of Bethlehem on that fateful night of long ago felt something of all these great emotions rushing through their beings as the angelic chorus sang and the angel spoke to them of the birth of our Savior. Oh, what a night that must have been! The deadly quiet of the Judean night sky was shattered by this angelic announcement of good news of great joy.

This good news contains a word about a marvelous love, a love that is truly beyond our comprehension. The greatest of human intellects cannot fathom the depths of this love. However, we can respond to this wonderful love, for it transcends our human frailty and our sin. This fact within itself is all but beyond our comprehension. As Paul affirmed in Romans 5:7-8 (NASB), "For one will hardly die for a righteous man; though perhaps for the good man someone would dare even to die. But God demonstrates His love toward us, in that while we were yet sinners, Christ died for us." How can this be, that God should love us in spite of our sin? There is nothing that we could ever do to deserve this wondrous love of God that has come to us abundantly in Jesus Christ, our Lord. All that God desires is our grateful devotion in response to his great love.

God's love not only is beyond our comprehension; it not only transcends our sin, but it also overcomes all human barriers whether real or contrived. It is higher than our petty differences and prejudices. This love knows no geographical or racial barriers. Frederick W. Faber expressed this idea well in his hymn, "There's a Wideness in God's Mercy":

> There's a wideness in God's mercy,
> Like the wideness of the sea;
> There's a kindness in his justice,
> Which is more than liberty.
>
> There is welcome for the sinner,
> And more graces for the good;
> There is mercy with the Savior;
> There is healing in his blood.
>
> But we make his love too narrow
> By false limits of our own;
> And we magnify his strictness
> With a zeal he will not own.
>
> For the love of God is broader
> Than the measure of man's mind;
> And the heart of the Eternal
> Is most wonderfully kind.

But God's love also transcends the best of human love and devotion. The noblest of human love is but a shooting star when compared with the eternal light of God's boundless love. Human love is but a poor imitation of the genuine thing, just a feeble copy of the original. There are no words to describe the greatness of God's love in comparison to human love.

This good news of great joy of which the angels spoke

that Judean night contains a word about the God of our confession. It tells us that he is a God who reveals himself to mankind. If our God were not a God of revelation, there would be no way that we could know him. Man cannot find God through intellect, ingenuity, or craftiness. Rather, man knows of God only what God reveals of himself to man. In the blessed event heralded by the angels to those Judean shepherds that glorious night, God has fully, finally, and completely revealed himself to mankind. The incarnation is the grandest miracle of all. Through this manner God has revealed to us that he is *not* just a transcendent God who has little or no interest in his creation. Rather he has great interest in the affairs of his creation. Because he has come to us in Jesus Christ, we know that he can sympathize with us in our weaknesses and our needs.

Our God is active in history, for it was the Holy Spirit who was at work in Mary to bring about the virgin conception of our Lord. This surely is a unique example of God working in the life of an individual. The incarnation itself means that God has broken into history. He has come to humanity on our own level. God has thrust himself into the arena of human activity in the person of Jesus Christ.

This God who is active in history is also one who gives of himself to his people. The greatest gift of all is God's unique gift of himself in Jesus Christ for the salvation of every person who will trust him. When we give our gifts to our loved ones at Christmastime, we should remember that the event which inspired the season of giving was God's gift of himself to us.

This good news of great joy of which the angels sang contains a word about worship. Adoration and worship surely are integral parts of the Christmas story, for we find that on at least four occasions people were worshiping Jesus soon after his birth. Matthew tells us that the Magi who came from the East worshiped him. The shepherds who witnessed the glorious angelic chorus came from the fields to behold and adore the wondrous Prince of peace. Simeon, the devout old man in the Temple, saw the young child and "took Him into his arms, and blessed God, and said,

> 'Now Lord, Thou dost let Thy bond-servant depart
> In peace, according to Thy word;
> For my eyes have seen Thy salvation,
> Which Thou hast prepared in the presence of all
>   peoples,
> A light of revelation to the Gentiles,
> And the glory of Thy people Israel' "
>   (Luke 2:28-32, NASB).

Anna, the prophetess, spoke of the babe as the redemption of Israel. (See Luke 2:38.)

Surely Christmas should be one of the most worshipful seasons of the year. However, we have almost succeeded in crowding Christ out of Christmas. I even heard some time ago of a lady who, as she viewed a nativity scene in the show window of a large city department store, said: "Well would you believe it! The church is even trying to horn in on Christmas." All too often, our Christmas celebrations turn out like the story of the little girl who attended her first Sunday School Christmas party. Her mother had coached her well. As she left home, her mother said: "Remember now, sweetheart, this is Jesus' birthday party." When the child returned home, her mother asked her about the party. The child replied: "It was a nice party mother, but Jesus never showed up." This may be a sad commentary on much that is done today under the guise of Christmas celebration—a party without the honored guest. Sadder still is the thought of commemorating Christ's birthday without an awareness of the presence of him whose incarnation we claim to celebrate—of him whose name the season bears. As we celebrate Christmas let us say with Robert Grant: "O worship the King, all glorious above, And gratefully sing his wonderful love" (from "O Worship the King").

13
The Compassion of God Incarnate

35 And Jesus was going about all the cities and the villages, teaching in their synagogues, and proclaiming the gospel of the kingdom, and healing every kind of disease and every kind of sickness.

36 And seeing the multitudes, He felt compassion for them, because they were distressed and downcast like sheep without a shepherd.

37 Then He said to His disciples, "The harvest is plentiful, but the workers are few.

38 "Therefore beseech the Lord of the harvest to send out workers into His harvest."

(Matthew 9:35-38, NASB)

17 Therefore, He had to be made like His brethren in all things, that He might become a merciful and faithful high priest in things pertaining to God, to make propitiation for the sins of the people.

18 For since He Himself was tempted in that which He has suffered, He is able to come to the aid of those who are tempted.

(Hebrews 2:17-18)

The clear teaching of the New Testament is that Jesus is God incarnate. That God has come in the flesh in the person of Jesus Christ is a cardinal Christian doctrine. In addition, we are told that, because of his sojourn in the flesh, our Lord is able to come to the aid of his people. There are a number of ways in which the New Testament sets forth this concept of Jesus. Perhaps the New Testament word which most clearly personifies this characteristic of Jesus is the one translated "compassion." Literally the word means to be touched in one's innermost being by the predicament of another. The word is used of Jesus many times in the Gospels, but it is used only in five different kinds of circumstances. A look at these different circumstances will alert us to those things which touched Jesus most deeply. As we view these episodes in the life of Jesus, let us ask ourselves if we are touched deeply by the same sort of circumstances which touched our Lord.

We should note also, as we view these episodes in the life of Jesus which moved him to compassion, that each time he was so touched he acted upon his feelings. You can be sure that each time the New Testament records that Jesus had compassion upon an individual or a group of people, he was going to act upon his compassion to take care of the particular need in question.

Jesus was moved to compassion by the pain of the people around him. He saw the sick and had compassion on them and healed them (Matt. 14:14). His heart went out to suffering masses of humanity to heal and ease their pain. In Matthew 20:29-34 an incident is recorded in which two blind men approached Jesus and asked him to have mercy on them. The crowd rebuked them and told them to be quiet. However, Jesus was moved with compassion by their condition, and he healed them. When he was confronted by those possessed by demons, Jesus responded by casting out the demons. He could not see suffering humanity without being moved with compassion for them.

He has not changed through the centuries. He still has compassion for his people. When his people are afflicted, so is he. He is moved by our pain and suffering.

Jesus was also moved to compassion by the world's sorrow. In Luke 7:13, it is recorded that he was moved to compassion by the sight of the widow of Nain as she followed the corpse of her only son. His was a life that was filled with sorrow and suffering, but when he saw it in the lives of others, he was moved to his depths. Though he did not raise to life all who died, and though he did not heal everyone who was sick, he certainly was compassionate toward people with these problems. How wonderful to know that we serve a Lord who is moved by our sorrows. He still is able to wipe away the tears from our eyes when we face sorrows and problems that seem to us to be insurmountable.

The third circumstance which called upon the compassion of our Lord was the hunger of those around him. The miracle of feeding the multitudes is recorded in all four Gospels. The sight of these poor, tired, and hungry souls was enough to call forth the power that was his. Often he did without food, but he was moved with compassion and performed one of his most notable miracles by feeding the hungry multitudes. Today the world is filled with hungry people who cry out to us for compassion. As followers of our Lord, we ought to be moved by the same things that called forth compassion from him. Do we feel that the hungry masses of the world have any right to cry out to us for help? All too often our response is the same as that of the disciples: "We have no more than five loaves and two fish" (Luke 9:13, NASB). Our Lord was able to make just a little go a long way. So it is today. If we all dedicate what we have to him, he can use it to his glory to bless the multitudes.

Another circumstance which moved our Lord to compassion was the loneliness of the outcast. In Mark 1:40-45, we find the account of a leper who called upon our Lord for help. The leper of Jesus' day lived a life of abandonment which was really a living death. He was an outcast from society. As far as society was concerned, God had placed this disease upon him as a punishment for his sins. He was driven away from family and friends. He was forced to live alone or with other lepers. He sought shelter in caves or abandoned places and was at the mercy of the world. When he saw someone coming, he was supposed to stand away from the path and call out "unclean, unclean" so those who passed by would avoid him. To come into contact with a leper was to render one unclean for seven days. People believed that the curse of the leper passed over to them when contact was made. However, when Jesus responded to the leper, he did not become unclean. Rather, the leper was cleansed. He rescued the leper from his loneliness. The cry of the leper in Mark 1:40 (NASB) is indeed instructive: "If You are willing, You can make me clean." He did not question Jesus' ability to cure him, but he did question his willingness. The rest of society had banished him to a life of loneliness. Why should Jesus respond any differently to him? What a lovely episode in the ministry of our Lord! There is so much loneliness in the world even today. We can share the compassion of Jesus with a lonely world if we are willing.

Jesus also was moved to compassion by the bewilderment of those to whom he ministered. The common people of his day were desperately longing for God, and the scribes and Pharisees, the so-called pillars of orthodoxy, had nothing to offer them. They had neither guidance, nor comfort, nor strength to give. In Matthew 9:36 (NASB), we find this statement: "And seeing the multitudes, He felt compassion for them, because they were distressed and downcast like sheep without a shepherd." The words Matthew used to describe the plight of the people here are vivid. The word translated "distressed" means to be vexed, harassed, or mangled. It was used to describe an animal carcass that has been mangled by wild beasts. Also it was used of someone who had been plundered and laid waste by robbers and left for dead. Beyond that, these poor people were vexed like sheep that had been sheared in the wintertime. "Downcast" means to lay prostrate. It could describe a person who was like this because of being intoxicated or because he had received a mortal wound. The picture here is of a shepherdless sheep that has been attacked by a wolf and laid low.

This is what Jesus saw as he looked at the people of his day, and he was moved to compassion by the sight. The Jewish leaders who should have been giving strength to the people were vexing them with subtle arguments about the law. When they should have been helping them stand upright, they were bowing them down with the intolerable burden of the scribal law. They were offering them a religion that was a burden rather than a support.

Christ has come to encourage rather than discourage. He has not come to weight us down but to lift us up. If our faith in him does not lift our burdens and give us strength, we have misunderstood the purpose of his coming.

He is God incarnate, and he has come to show us what God is like. Beyond a doubt we can say that God is compassion. He has come to the aid of his people, and he stands ready to strengthen us for our sojourn.

14
Our Elder Brother

11 For both He who sanctifies and those who are sanctified are all from one Father; for which reason He is not ashamed to call them brethren,

12 saying, "I will proclaim Thy name to My brethren, In the midst of the congregation I will sing Thy praise."

13 And again, "I will put My trust in Him." And again, "Behold, I and the children whom God has given Me."

14 Since then the children share in flesh and blood, He Himself likewise also partook of the same, that through death he might render powerless him who had the power of death, that is, the devil;

15 and might deliver those who through fear of death were subject to slavery all their lives.

16 For assuredly He does not give help to angels, but He gives help to the seed of Abraham.

17 Therefore, He had to be made like His brethren in all things, that He might become a merciful and faithful high priest in things pertaining to God, to make propitiation for the sins of the people.

18 For since He Himself was tempted in that which He has suffered, He is able to come to the aid of those who are tempted.

(Hebrews 2:11-18, NASB)

The Epistle to the Hebrews has as much to say about Christ as any other New Testament document. The writer was concerned with proving that Jesus was superior to anyone or anything in the Jewish religious system. He argued that Jesus was superior to angels, to Moses, and to the Levitical priests. In so doing he presented Jesus as the fulfillment of the Jewish high priesthood. He is the ultimate high priest who offers the supreme sacrifice for his people.

In this passage leading into the discussion of Jesus as high priest, the writer uses several descriptive phrases to tell his readers what Jesus has done for them and how he has done it. The descriptions in this passage are centered around the concept of Jesus as our brother. Several important precepts grow out of this spiritual relationship with Jesus as our elder brother.

As our brother, Jesus is closely identified with our humanity. The writer begins the passage by affirming that our Lord and those he came to save are from one Father. Now the writer was not trying to say that Jesus was a created being. He has already affirmed that Jesus was the agent in the divine creative process (Heb. 1:2). The inference here simply is that Jesus was closely identified with humanity. Indeed, the clear inference of this passage is that it was essential for him to partake of humanity or that he should be a suffering man. There could not be a clearer reference to the incarnation than this. Our Lord redeemed and sanctified mankind and is not ashamed to call them his brothers. This relationship was not forced upon him. Rather, he willingly identified himself with mankind. There was in the work of redemption a oneness between him and humanity. Hence it was necessary that he become man.

There may be here an extension of the prophetic idea of corporate personality. In neither the Old Testament nor the New Testament does the individual stand alone. He is always thought of as being a part of the larger group. The son is an extension of his father and as such is a part of the family unit, then of the clan or tribe, and then of the total human community.

This concept of corporate personality is most difficult for twentieth-century Americans to grasp. We are so oriented toward the individual that we have trouble with the group dynamic. Our society is by and large the product of the rugged individualism of the American frontier. We are as polarized toward the individual in our society as the ancients were toward the group. Many people today want to do their own thing without regard to the effect or consequences of their actions on others.

For the writer of Hebrews, the Savior of mankind is one who arises out of the group and is united with the group in experience. He is not ashamed to call us his brothers. What a marvelous concept this is, and what far-reaching implications it has for Christians! Not only is Jesus our exalted Savior and Lord, but he is our elder brother who knows our weaknesses and our infirmities. He has shared with us in a common humanity.

As our elder brother, he has canceled the power of the devil. Through his death, our Lord rendered powerless the one who had the power of death. The writer has affirmed that the devil introduced death into the world and is responsible for its long and melancholy reign in the world. This does not affirm that the devil has the power to inflict death in particular instances. The writer was speaking generically rather than in specific terms. Death was a part of Satan's dominion. He introduced death. He seduced man from God, and brought on all the woes that accompany death. He also made death terrible. Through his reign of sin death became terrible, a thing to be dreaded and feared.

Because of what Jesus has done as our elder brother in

his common humanity, we have been delivered from the fear of death. Our writer viewed this fear of death as a bondage and as slavery. Those who live in the bondage of the fear of death are like those who are held prisoners all of their lives without any hope of being released. But thanks be to God, our elder brother has come and through his work of redemption has given help to the seed of Abraham. He has broken the bonds of death and loosed us from its terror and bondage.

Not only has Christ loosed us from the terror and bondage of death, his victory over the grave assures us of the coming destruction of the dominion of death. Surely this grand and benevolent undertaking, which anticipates the annihilation of death, should make us all profoundly grateful.

Because of what Jesus has done as our elder brother, death should hold no terror or despair for the child of God. Through his resurrection, our Lord has overcome this terrible enemy and has broken the bonds of the grave. So we can say with Paul: "'O death, where is your victory? O death, where is your sting?' . . . thanks be to God, who gives us the victory through our Lord Jesus Christ" (1 Cor. 15:55,57, NASB).

Jesus can sympathize with us in all of our problems because of his identification with mankind as our elder brother. The text literally says that he can *feel* with us. He has stood where we stand. He has been tempted as we are. He has suffered beyond anything we can comprehend. He did these things not only to gain insight into the human situation, but also that we might realize he *does* have a genuine insight into our situation. From the human perspective, then, it was necessary that our Savior should identify himself with us as our elder brother.

Because of our human limitations it is all but impossible

for us to understand another person's sorrows unless we have been through the same kind of experience. A person without a trace of nerves has no conception of the tortures of nervousness. One who knows no pain cannot understand the person whose life is never free from pain. Before we can truly sympathize with another, we must experience the same things they are experiencing. The writer of Hebrews says that this is precisely what Jesus did as our elder brother. He took on the afflictions and the infirmities of our flesh and suffered and was tempted even as we are.

Our Lord truly can sympathize with us, and because he can, he can help us in every difficulty. As the writer has said: "For since He Himself was tempted in that which He has suffered, He is able to come to the aid of those who are tempted" (Heb. 2:18, NASB).

Jesus truly is our elder brother in the sense that he has been in our place and is able to lead us safely through life's experiences. What more could we ask?

15
Christc
Our Mediator

For there is one God, and one mediator also between God and men, the man Christ Jesus.

(1 Timothy 2:5, NASB)

But now He has obtained a more excellent ministry, by as much as He is also the mediator of a better covenant, which has been enacted on better promises.

(Hebrews 8:6, NASB)

And for this reason He is the mediator of a new covenant, in order that since a death has taken place for the redemption of the transgressions that were committed under the first covenant, those who have been called may receive the promise of the eternal inheritance.

(Hebrews 9:15, NASB)

and to Jesus, the mediator of a new covenant, and to the sprinkled blood, which speaks better than the blood of Abel.

(Hebrews 12:24, NASB)

The basic idea in the word translated "mediator" is that of a neutral third party who can serve as an umpire in a dispute. In the Old Testament, when the Law was given, Moses was the one through whom it was mediated. Later the high priest was the one who approached God on behalf of the people. He was considered to be a mediator, especially on the Day of Atonement when he approached the holy of holies and sprinkled the blood of the atoning sacrifice on the mercy seat.

In the New Testament, Jesus is called mediator only four times, once in 1 Timothy and three times in Hebrews. His mediatorial activity can be detected often in the New Testament, but he is called a mediator only in these four places.

In what sense can our Lord be spoken of as a mediator, and what does he do as our mediator? Because of his nature as the God-man, he can be called our mediator. He was God of very God, and he was truly man. He contained in his person all that was needed to be the perfect mediator. The mystery of all mysteries confronts us in Jesus Christ. We cannot explain the miracle of the incarnation; we can only affirm it. Any other miracle known to man pales into insignificance beside the incarnation. How could the infinite God limit himself to become finite man? This mystery surely is beyond our understanding. However, precisely because of this miracle there is one who acts as our mediator. In his person he mediates God, and he mediates man. He is not a third party go-between. He is not half-God and half-man. He is no third kind. In his person resides God and man. Because of this he perfectly represents both. In his book entitled *The Mediator,* Emil Brunner has given us a classic definition for Jesus' work as mediator. He says: "He is indeed the Incarnate Word, in Him and in His being God is the One who has come to us. Thus in His very Nature the gulf between God and man has been bridged. He Himself is the bridge which God throws across to us, over which God comes to us."[1] Jesus is not one who is *between* God and man. The word *between* is not to be found in the Greek text of 1 Timothy 2:5. Rather, he overcomes that betweenness that has existed in God and man's relationship.

As our mediator, Jesus does at least three things. First, he brings God to man. Through his coming into the world, he shows us what God is really like. From him we learn that God is love, and that he desires that no person should perish, but that all should come to repentance. In what greater way could God show his concern for mankind than by becoming a man and dwelling among men? Charles Wesley expressed it well in the first four lines of his hymn, "Love Divine, All Loves Excelling."

> Love divine, all loves excelling,
> Joy of heav'n to earth come down;
> Fix in us thy humble dwelling;
> All thy faithful mercies crown.

We cannot fathom what he did for us. We cannot know the love he had for us, but the eternal God came into time and space and allowed himself to be limited by it. The all-powerful sovereign of the universe stepped off his majestic throne to be crowned with thorns on a cruel cross. As our mediator, he brings God to mankind.

As our mediator, he also represents mankind to God. Just as surely as he is God, he is also man. He accepted the limitations of a man so that we might know that God understands and is sympathetic with our plight. He feels with us because he is one with us in our humanity. He is our perfect representative who brings mankind to God.

As our mediator, he also brings into effect a new and better covenant. Three times in the epistle to the Hebrews, Christ is spoken as the mediator of this covenant. Each time this concept is mentioned, the author of Hebrews explains the covenant which Jesus mediates in terms of the old covenant made with Israel. In each case the writer uses a different adjective to describe this covenant. The first time he refers to it as a better or superior covenant. This is true, affirms the writer of Hebrews, because if the first covenant had been superior, it would not have been replaced by the second covenant. Second, he says that the covenant which Christ mediates is a new kind of covenant. The first was a covenant of law; the second is a covenant of grace. The third time, he speaks of the covenant as new in point of time. As God's plan for his creation unfolded, it was necessary that the old covenant of law be replaced by a new covenant of grace so that mankind might be brought into a right relation with God in Christ.

What does the mediatorial activity of Christ mean to us as Christians? In the first place, it means that we can know more fully the character of God. We can know God through his self-revelation in Jesus Christ. Had he not come to us in the incarnation to reveal himself to us we could not know God. But because of what he has done for us as mediator we can understand better the character of God.

Because of what God has done in Christ as our mediator, man can find his true destiny in the plan of God. Man was created for service to God and fellowship with God. That purpose can be realized fully only in Jesus Christ.

We have an advocate with the Father who is Jesus Christ our mediator. He was tempted as we are, yet without sin. He is able to sympathize with us in our trials and to save us from sin. What more could we ask?

Note

1. Emil Brunner *The Mediator* (Philadelphia: The Westminster Press, nd), Copyright W.L. Jenkins, nd, pp. 490-91.

16
He Emptied Himself for Us

5 Have this attitude in yourselves which was also in Christ Jesus,

6 who, although He existed in the form of God, did not regard equality with God a thing to be grasped,

7 but emptied Himself, taking the form of a bond-servant, and being made in the likeness of men.

8 And being found in appearance as a man, He humbled Himself by becoming obedient to the point of death, even death on a cross.

9 Therefore also God highly exalted Him, and bestowed on Him the name which is above every name,

10 that at the name of Jesus every knee should bow, of those who are in heaven, and on earth, and under the earth,

11 and that every tongue should confess that Jesus Christ is Lord, to the glory of God the Father.

(Philippians 2:5-11, NASB)

Paul exhorted his readers to be united in effort and in action. He urged them not to do anything from the wrong motivation, but rather to act with humility. They were to be responsive to the needs and interests of others rather than thinking solely of their own affairs. At this point, Paul proceeded to make one of the loftiest statements about Christ to be found anywhere in the New Testament. With the deft stroke of a master artist, Paul painted a vivid verbal picture of the glory that belonged to the cosmic Christ prior to the incarnation. Then in verse 7, Paul affirmed that Christ emptied himself. This word would have been used to describe the action of one who poured all of the contents out of a vessel.

We well may ask the question: Of what did Christ empty himself? To be sure he divested himself of the prerogatives that were his prior to the incarnation as Deity. He was willing to leave the crown of glory for a crown of thorns. He willingly exchanged the throne of Deity for the ignominious death on the cross. His was a voluntary emptying, for Paul indicated that he did not look upon his estate in glory as something to which he should cling. Rather, he was willing to leave this blessed estate to be born as a baby in Bethlehem's manger to live, suffer, and die as a man.

> What wondrous love is this,
> O my soul, O my soul!
> What wondrous love is this,
> O my soul!
> What wondrous love is this
> That caused the Lord of bliss
> To bear the dreadful curse
>   for my soul, for my soul,
> To bear the dreadful curse for my soul.
>   (American folk hymn)

The one reason for this self-emptying is his wondrous love for mankind. He did not come to sojourn among men because man was worthy of his presence. His sojourn on earth was more than just a noble, divine experiment to satisfy the curiosity of God concerning man's response to his revealing activity. He came to us because he loved us in spite of our sin and because of the helplessness of our plight.

The form of the verb used here for the act of self-emptying is such that it is possible to see here a reference to Christ's entrance into the world as a babe in Bethlehem's manger. If so, this is for mankind a marvelous theological tribute to the Christmas story. For it tells us that our Lord was willing to leave the counsels of Deity in the realm of glory and come to earth, so that he might identify himself with mankind.

In this beautiful hymn on the person of our Lord, Paul has summed up in a marvelous way the results of this self-emptying. First Paul stated that Christ "humbled himself." This phrase describes a quality of character that was degrading and was to be despised as far as the proud Greek man was concerned. For the Greek writers, *humility* was a term of derision, a vice rather than a virtue. A slave or perhaps a woman might display humility, but never a Greek man. He was proud, arrogant, and self-sufficient—very much the image of the so-called "macho" man today. He looked disdainfully on anyone who displayed a spirit of humility. However, the Christian writers in general and Paul in particular took this word and made it a character trait of beauty, dignity, and grace. It is interesting also to note that Paul did not describe this quality as something that was forced upon our Lord. Rather, he described it as a life-style which our Lord chose for himself. His was a voluntary humility and self-abasement.

Paul states also that our Lord was obedient. The word literally means to hear instruction, understand it, and then take action upon the instruction. Throughout the period of his incarnation, our Lord was unswervingly obedient to the will of the Father. There was never a moment when he veered from the path set for him by the Father. The culmination of his life of obedience can be seen at Calvary. Not only did he forsake his existence as glorified Deity for the humility of the incarnation, but as a man he died. He turned his back on everything that man calls glory. He rejected the fame that some would have given him as a miracle worker. He refused the kingdoms of this world when offered to him on Satan's terms. Instead, he accepted the most shameful death of his day. Crucifixion was reserved for thieves, murderers, and insurrectionists. So abhorrent was this form of death that the Old Testament pronounced a curse on anyone who died in this way. (See Deut. 21:23.)

Our Lord was not just obedient unto death. The preposition which Paul used here indicates degree or measure. In other words, he was obedient to the dying point. Being obedient until death is not as difficult if death comes quickly. However, when one is put to death by degrees, obedience can be a supreme test. Our Lord's death was by a slow, painful method, and he was obedient to the very point of dying. In other words, Paul wanted his readers to know that our Lord never breathed a disobedient breath, but he followed his Father's will to the very last.

Perhaps the supreme result of our Lord's self-emptying is his exaltation, which according to this scriptural hymn came about because of his death on the cross. When the word "wherefore" (Phil. 2:9, KJV) appears in Paul's writings, the reader is alerted to the fact that what follows is based upon what has just been written. In other words, Paul asserts that our Lord's exaltation is based on his death of humiliation. The result of his exaltation is the fact that God has given to him the name that is above every name.

The response to all of this is that every knee shall bow before him, and every tongue shall confess that he is Lord. This is a succinct description of worship in its purest form. He is worthy of our praise and adoration whether it be at Christmas or throughout the year. When we approach the manger scene at Christmastime, let us remember that this was not his beginning. Rather, it was his entrance into the world of men. It was the starting point of his pilgrimage of self-emptying, humility, and obedience which would ultimately lead him to Calvary.

> Infant holy,
> Infant lowly,
> For his bed a cattle stall;
> Oxen lowing,
> Little knowing
> Christ the Babe is Lord of all.
> Swift are winging
> Angels singing,
> Noels ringing,
> Tidings bringing:
> Christ the Babe is Lord of All.
>
> Flocks were sleeping,
> Shepherds keeping
> Vigil till the morning new
> Saw the glory,
> Heard the story,
> Tidings of a gospel true.
> Thus rejoicing,
> Free from sorrow,
> Praises voicing
> Greet the morrow:
> Christ the Babe was born for you![1]

Note

1. Words, Polish Carol; paraphrased by Edith M. G. Reed, ©1925, *Kingsway Carol Book*. Used by permission Evans Brothers, Ltd.